CHOSEN TO BUILD

Guiding Words of Biblical Wisdom
for Kingdom Builders

ASHLEY ENNIS

ISBN: 9798840574263

With Love,
To Mom & Dad

I'm so grateful for you both. Love you more than I have the
words to say. Thank you for sharing your wisdom and for
teaching us all how to walk in it.

"Wisdom is the principal thing; therefore get wisdom:
and with all thy getting get understanding." ~Proverbs 4:7

CONTENTS

"King Solomon made himself a chariot of the wood of Lebanon. He made the pillars thereof of silver, the bottom thereof of gold, the covering of it of purple, the midst thereof being paved with love, for the daughters of Jerusalem. Go forth, O ye daughters of Zion, and behold king Solomon with the crown wherewith his mother crowned him in the day of his espousals, and in the day of the gladness of his heart."

-Song of Solomon 3:9-11

KINGDOM BUILDERS

King Solomon was a builder. The Lord chose Solomon from among all of King David's children to build His temple. This is true for you, as well. You are chosen. Chosen for heaven. Chosen to do great and mighty things for the Kingdom of God. Chosen to win the lost. Chosen to make disciples. Chosen to encourage. Chosen to build. Chosen to do the thing God has purposed for you to do.

Proverbs 29:18 says that without vision the people perish, but it is also true that without determination the people give up and quit. You may be in a place right now where you feel the call to complete something great for the kingdom and you can even see the vision before you, but you are unsure how to turn the vision into reality. You just aren't sure how to get from seeing to doing. Maybe you are in the doing, but it feels more like the muck of day-to-day. Somehow you thought building your vision would be glamorous or perhaps you didn't think there would be so many days of struggle and you feel like giving up. What does it take to keep going? Where does the drive come from to finish the work you have started?

The Jews were astonished at Jesus. His ways were like an unexpected tsunami in their customs and experiences. Mark 7:37 tells us they were astonished because, "…he hath done all things well." There is a move the Spirit wants to do in our lives. A call to excellence and productivity in the people of God. That call you feel to do for the kingdom is not simply a suggestion, it is a pull from heaven to do all things well. John 15:5 says, "I am the vine, ye are the branches: He that abideth in me, and I in him, the same bringeth forth much fruit: for without me ye can do nothing." The call to bring forth fruit is a precious breeze moving across God's children. You are reading this because you too hear the Lord calling you to greater things for His name's sake. The world offers many tools to accomplish our goals, but tools will never be the catalyst to bearing fruit. Our ability to do everything we are called to do comes from abiding in the One who called us. Our strategies and the meat of the assignment comes from our daily encounters with Jesus.

Solomon was given a great assignment, but the privilege he received to be chosen came with a warning, the book of Luke tells us, "for unto whomsoever much is given, of him shall be much required" (12:48). As King David was passing down the torch of leadership to his son, he did not mince words about what was expected of the soon-to-be King:

> And of all my sons, (for the Lord hath given me many sons,) he hath chosen Solomon my son to sit upon the throne of the kingdom of the Lord over Israel. And he said unto me, Solomon thy son, he shall build my house and my courts: for I have chosen him to be my son, and I will be his father. Moreover I will establish his kingdom for ever, if he be constant to do my commandments and my judgments, as at this day. Now therefore in the sight of all Israel the congregation of the Lord, and in the audience of our God, keep and seek for all the commandments of the Lord your God: that ye may possess this good land, and leave it for an inheritance for your children after you for ever. And thou, Solomon my son,

know thou the God of thy father, and serve him with a perfect heart and with a willing mind: for the Lord searcheth all hearts, and understandeth all the imaginations of the thoughts: if thou seek him, he will be found of thee; but if thou forsake him, he will cast thee off for ever. Take heed now; for the Lord hath chosen thee to build an house for the sanctuary: be strong, and do it.

-1 Chronicles 28:5-10

We can break this moment down into two categories: what God promised and Solomon's responsibility. Within that passage, God identifies what He would do and what Solomon should do. Notice Solomon's list is longer, but God's list is divine. Solomon's list hinges on relationship with the God who created him and called him, God's list simply requires Him to be who He is- the Creator of the Universe who makes all things possible.

What God Does	*What Solomon Does*
-Choose Solomon	*-Build God's House and Courts*
-Establish Solomon's Kingdom	*-Be Constant*
-Search Hearts	*-Do God's Commandments and Judgments*
-Understand Imaginations	*-Keep and Seek God's Commandments*
	-Possess the Land
	-Know God
	-Serve God with a Perfect Heart and a Willing Mind
	-Be Strong and Do It

The stakes were high for Solomon. To keep the blessings of God it was up to him to fall madly in love with the lover of his soul. It wasn't, however, just the initial falling in love that God wanted, much like a marriage that develops over time, what God wanted was a lasting relationship with Solomon. He wanted to grow with him and be the source of his strength all the days of his life. Perhaps the most telling set of instructions for Solomon, the keystone to the call on his life, can be found in the word *if:* "if he be constant to do my commandments and my judgments, as at this day." The Lord told Solomon up front, before he became king, before he built the temple, before the wealth and the wisdom, that his future was dependent upon his constant desire to seek God in every stage and situation throughout his life and with the same fervency he had as on the day it all began. He was expected to know God, keep His commandments, and serve Him with a perfect heart and a willing mind. He was expected to be constant.

To be constant is to be unshakeable and unwavering; to set a pace and keep it. A walk like this requires wisdom, a trait Solomon was given in a large dose because he had asked God for wisdom to rule His people well:

> Now, O Lord God, let thy promise unto David my father be established: for thou hast made me king over a people like the dust of the earth in multitude. Give me now wisdom and knowledge, that I may go out and come in before this people: for who can judge this thy people, that is so great?
>
> -2 Chronicles 1:9-10

Solomon's request pleased God because it proved he had a heart to serve the Lord by serving others well. God gifted him wisdom so that he was "wiser than all men" (1 Kings 4:31). He was given the most important tool needed to build and lead Israel. It was the largest jewel in his crown and the marker by which he was known. The Queen of Sheba traveled far and wide just to sit at Solomon's feet and hear his words. He spoke proverbs and sang songs by the thousands. He was full of knowledge, but wisdom isn't just knowledge, it is how to apply knowledge in relationships. This was pivotal for the new king, if he would maintain His relationship with the Lord, wisdom would serve him and generations after him, but if he became complacent in his relationship, wisdom would destroy him.

Fast-forward to the end of Solomon's reign and you will find a king who was wise, but who did not heed his father's warning about relationship:

> But king Solomon loved many strange women, together with the daughter of Pharaoh, women of the Moabites, Ammonites, Edomites, Zidonians, and Hittites: Of the nations concerning which the Lord said unto the children of Israel, Ye shall not go in to them, neither shall they come in unto you: for surely they will turn away your heart after their gods: Solomon clave unto these in love. And he had seven hundred wives, princesses, and three hundred concubines: and his wives turned away his heart. For it came to pass, when Solomon was old, that his wives turned away his heart after other gods: and his heart was not perfect with the Lord his God, as was the heart

of David his father…And Solomon did evil in the sight of the Lord, and went not fully after the Lord, as did David his father. Then did Solomon build an high place for Chemosh, the abomination of Moab, in the hill that is before Jerusalem, and for Molech, the abomination of the children of Ammon. And likewise did he for all his strange wives, which burnt incense and sacrificed unto their gods. And the Lord was angry with Solomon, because his heart was turned from the Lord God of Israel, which had appeared unto him twice, And had commanded him concerning this thing, that he should not go after other gods: but he kept not that which the Lord commanded. Wherefore the Lord said unto Solomon, Forasmuch as this is done of thee, and thou hast not kept my covenant and my statutes, which I have commanded thee, I will surely rend the kingdom from thee, and will give it to thy servant.

-1 Kings 11:1-11

What a mess. Can you imagine? Solomon trying to please all those women. I'm sure most spouses have their hands full trying to please just one person, much less trying to make sure all those wives from all those countries each had their own culture and religion represented. This chosen servant of the King of kings, the one who was called to build God's temple and rule His people, allowed himself to be the builder of temples for false gods, the gods of his wives and his concubines, the very people the Lord warned him about from the beginning. He allowed the heart he was given to serve God to become a heart that cleaved to unholy relationships. How many times have we done this? How many times have the people of God chosen to love this world and cherish sin with the very heart that Jesus created within us to love Him? Wisdom is only wise in the context of holiness. Solomon did not finish his race well, somewhere along the way he stopped trying to please God and began living to please others. He turned away from his first love and God was not okay with it. He didn't overlook the sin. He didn't ignore Solomon's transgression. God stuck to His Word from the beginning and judged His chosen one with the same measure as He would have anyone else. There was no favoritism. There was no special loophole. Solomon was accountable for his actions, and they did not go unnoticed. I have no doubt he was given chance after chance, perhaps even a thousand chances, one for each wife and concubine, but this was an Old Testament way of doing things and the Lord had had enough. It would be his children that would suffer most from his mistakes. The kingdom would be divided, and Israel would always struggle to maintain kings that would do right in the eyes of the Lord.

What is pure wisdom?

James 3:17 tells us, "But the wisdom that is from above is first pure, then peaceable, gentle, and easy to be intreated, full of mercy and good fruits, without partiality, and without hypocrisy." True wisdom sounds like Jesus.
Jesus is pure.
Jesus is peaceable.
Jesus is gentle.
Jesus is easy to be intreated.

Jesus is full of mercy and good fruits.

Jesus is without partiality.

Jesus is without hypocrisy.

Our definition for wisdom throughout this book will always be in the context of relationship. Relationship with Jesus and relationship with others. Isn't this why you are here? Isn't this why you were chosen? You are a builder in a kingdom built on souls and those "that winneth souls is wise"(Proverbs 11:30). According to *Vines Complete Expository Dictionary*, wisdom is full of elements we can grab a hold of.

Wisdom is:

-A process of attainment and not an accomplishment

-A life lived projecting the fear of God and the blessings of God

-The application of wisdom in life

-A technical skill or special ability in fashioning something

-The knowledge and ability to make the right choices at the right time

-A desire to follow and imitate God as He reveals Himself

Wisdom is something we can attain, project, apply, fashion, choose, and follow. Wisdom, much like building a house, is an action. Without wisdom we run the risk of being like the woman who tears down her own house with the choices she makes, "Every wise woman buildeth her house: but the foolish plucketh it down with her hands" (Proverbs 14:1).

Jesus was a people person, and even now He says to us, "Ask. Seek. Knock." He wants us to be successful in the building of our lives, families, businesses, ministries, and everything we set our hands to- this is what the Kingdom of God consists of, our lives and our constant commitment to going about our Father's business. Knowing this, we will mine for wisdom from the quarry of the Lord, "In whom are hid all the treasures of wisdom and knowledge" (Colossians 2:3). We will look to Him as our primary example, an example He shares with us freely.

Jesus hung on a cross so we could be with Him in heaven for eternity. For those of us who have caught the revelation of redemption, we are now responsible for sharing that good news with others in a way that honors God as the treasure that He is.

Solomon was wise for a season and did many great things in that season, but he lost his way one bad choice at a time. God was looking to walk with Solomon the way He walked with David, but instead, He was placed on the back burner as Solomon ran after his own fleshly desires. What we do matters, and it matters greatly. We have the opportunity to apply lessons from the Word directly to our choices and watch relationships flourish as a result. When we seek God first, with a perfect heart and a willing mind, we will lead others to the same joy we have found.

Principles of Wisdom

According to the Word, there is a spirit of wisdom that we as followers of Christ may ask for, "That the God of our Lord Jesus Christ, the Father of glory, may give unto you the spirit of wisdom and revelation in the knowledge of him"(Ephesians 1:17). This is not something we can give to ourselves, but our heavenly Father is able to gift us this treasure from His own heart as we grow in relationship with Him. Perhaps Solomon's relationship with God could have been enough if he had allowed it. The one God called to be King took on a lot of extra stress and extra distraction that took his focus off the job he was given.

Let's finish our race well, asking for wisdom that sustains us until the end. Mature Christians strive to do all things well, after all, Jesus left us His name. He wants us to use it with faith, excellence, and integrity. In this book, you will delve into guiding words found throughout the book of Proverbs to aid you on your mission to be the builder you were called to be, whether it is in your home, place of business, community, or ministry. Wherever it is, Jesus wants you to be successful and productive. You were chosen to build.

Jesus, I thank you for the blessings in my life and the relationships You have established for me. I pray for a spirit of wisdom to run through my words and actions. Lord, out of Your mouth comes knowledge and understanding, so I pray You speak over me as I am constant in my seeking of You. Your thoughts and Your ways are so much higher than mine and it is Your heart I desire. Thank you for giving to me freely as I endeavor to help build Your kingdom. Help me to walk in obedience with a perfect heart and a willing mind. I thank you in advance for the liberal gift of wisdom and the fruit that will come as I apply it where Your Spirit leads. It is in Your name I pray. Amen

"For the Lord giveth wisdom: out of his mouth cometh knowledge and understanding." Proverbs 2:6

"If any of you lack wisdom, let him ask of God, that giveth to all men liberally, and upbraideth not; and it shall be given him." James 1:5

"But the manifestation of the Spirit is given to every man to profit withal. For to one is given by the Spirit the word of wisdom; to another the word of knowledge by the same Spirit;" 1 Corinthians 12:7-8

"For my thoughts are not your thoughts, neither are your ways my ways, saith the Lord." Isaiah 55:8

Reflection Questions:

1. Where are you partnering with God to build?

    ____

    ____

    ____

    ____

2. Where could you use wisdom in your relationships?

    ____

    ____

    ____

    ____

3. In what ways do you seek Jesus in your building?

    ____

    ____

    ____

    ____

4. Where do you turn for advice?

    ____

    ____

    ____

    ____

5. How do you share the good news of the gospel?

    ____

    ____

    ____

    ____

-Solomon was chosen among all of David's children to be King of Israel and build His temple.

-With this calling Solomon was given guidance to stay in relationship with God and to consistently seek Him with "a perfect heart and a willing mind."

-Solomon asked for and was given the gift of wisdom to serve in his position of leadership. He used it well for a season, but eventually neglected the Word of the Lord and allowed his heart to be turned away from God. His relationships with women overtook his relationship with God, causing him to worship idols.

-You too have been called to build God's kingdom and have been given the same command as Solomon- to consistently seek Jesus with "a perfect heart and a willing mind."

-Jesus is the fount of true wisdom, and it is through our relationship with Him that we help build the Kingdom of God. Without relationship, we can do nothing.

-Wisdom allows us to successfully build and maintain relationships with others, an important element in sharing and living out the gospel of Jesus Christ.

-Jesus wants you to be successful in your calling. You were chosen to build.

DILIGENCE: THE SEEKING

On what had to be one of the scariest days of their lives, Mary and Joseph frantically searched for their missing son. Jesus was nowhere to be found and the hunt was on. Time must have both stood still and raced by as these two parents turned over every rock and knocked on every door in hopes of seeing the face of their Jesus looking back at them. Finally, after three long days, there He was- their child, their Savior, their responsibility, and their joy, sitting in the temple changing the world with His words:

> Now his parents went to Jerusalem every year at the feast of the passover. And when he was twelve years old, they went up to Jerusalem after the custom of the feast. And when they had fulfilled the days, as they returned, the child Jesus tarried behind in Jerusalem; and Joseph and his mother knew not of it. But they, supposing him to have been in the company, went a day's journey; and they sought him among their kinsfolk and acquaintance. And when they found him not, they turned back again to Jerusalem, seeking him. And it came to pass, that after three days they found him in the temple, sitting in the midst of the doctors, both hearing them, and asking them questions. And all that heard him were astonished at his understanding and answers. And when they saw him, they were amazed: and his mother said unto him, Son, why hast thou thus dealt with us? behold, thy father and I have sought thee sorrowing. And he said unto them, How

is it that ye sought me? wist ye not that I must be about my Father's business? And they understood not the saying which he spake unto them. And he went down with them, and came to Nazareth, and was subject unto them: but his mother kept all these sayings in her heart. And Jesus increased in wisdom and stature, and in favour with God and man.

-Luke 2:41-52

As a parent, I love this passage. The amount of grace God gives us by this example is almost unbelievable. Here, He is telling us that even Mary and Joseph made mistakes. They lost Jesus. If they had thrown up their hands and said "Oh, well!" we would question God's judgment for His choice of authority figures, but Mary and Joseph cared about Jesus. They cared about His safety, and they wanted to find Him, so they did what any of us would have done…they searched until they saw Him face to face.

When Mary and Joseph spoke with their son in the temple, questioning why He would run off the way He did, Jesus simply said "How is it that you sought me?"

Today, Jesus is asking us, "How is it that you sought me?"

Jesus had not been easy to find, but Mary and Joseph were diligent. They didn't give up until they found their child. They searched high and low until they had Him in their sight. Hebrews 11:6 tells us, "But without faith it is impossible to please him: for he that cometh to God must believe that he is, and that he is a rewarder of them that diligently seek him."

To be diligent is to be steady, constant, and attentive in accomplishing a task.

Steady. Constant. Attentive.

Jesus had been about His Father's business. There were things He needed to do while in Jerusalem and He was not yet ready to leave. There are things we need to do as we go about our Father's business. To please God, we must take our faith in Jesus seriously. It isn't something that we can pick up and put down as we choose, but it is a steady, constant, and attentive way of life that leads us and others into a relationship with our Savior.

The book of Proverbs has much to say about the topic of diligence:

-"He becometh poor that dealeth with a slack hand: but the hand of the diligent maketh rich." Proverbs 10:4

-"The hand of the diligent shall bear rule: but the slothful shall be under tribute." Proverbs 12:24

-"He that diligently seeketh good procureth favour: but he that seeketh mischief, it shall come unto him." Proverbs 11:27

-"The soul of the sluggard desireth, and hath nothing: but the soul of the diligent shall be made fat." Proverbs 13:4

-"Seest thou a man diligent in his business? he shall stand before kings; he shall not stand before mean men." Proverbs 22:29

From these verses we learn:

Diligence leads to wealth.
Diligence leads to authority.
Diligence leads to favor.
Diligence leads to abundance.
Diligence leads to success.

Wisdom is a process of attainment, and in this process, we must have a plan of attack. Matthew 11:12 tells us, "And from the days of John the Baptist until now the kingdom of heaven suffereth violence, and the violent take it by force." In other words, we can't afford to be spiritual wimps with no sense of direction and in no hurry to get anywhere. There are things we need to do while we are here. God is building His kingdom *in you* and *through you*, but He won't do it without your permission or your participation. The blueprint we use to build is always the Word of God.

Peter writes to us about the importance of building on our faith and the promises we have in God:

> According as his divine power hath given unto us all things that pertain unto life and godliness, through the knowledge of him that hath called us to glory and virtue: Whereby are given unto us exceeding great and precious promises: that by these ye might be partakers of the divine nature, having escaped the corruption that is in the world through lust. And beside this, giving all diligence, add to your faith virtue; and to virtue knowledge; And to knowledge temperance; and to temperance patience; and

to patience godliness; And to godliness brotherly kindness; and to brotherly kindness charity. For if these things be in you, and abound, they make you that ye shall neither be barren nor unfruitful in the knowledge of our Lord Jesus Christ. But he that lacketh these things is blind, and cannot see afar off, and hath forgotten that he was purged from his old sins. Wherefore the rather, brethren, give diligence to make your calling and election sure: for if ye do these things, ye shall never fall: For so an entrance shall be ministered unto you abundantly into the everlasting kingdom of our Lord and Savior Jesus Christ.

-2 Peter 1:3-11

We have been called into glory and virtue through the knowledge of Jesus Christ. This knowledge helps us escape the world and partake of Christ's divine nature. 1 Corinthians 2:16 instructs us that we "have the mind of Christ." What an amazing life! We get to be a part of a supernatural change that takes place as we are transformed into the image of Jesus on this earth (2 Corinthians 3:18). As if this weren't enough, Peter is telling us this is just the basic model- the factory setting. We have the ability to do even more for the Kingdom of God by choosing to add and benefit others. So much of the maturity that we walk in is up to us. What are you willing to set aside so the name of Jesus can be exalted? Hate, jealousy, bitterness, and so much more are a work of the flesh that can be crucified as we choose to walk in the Spirit.

The Word tells us:

-To your faith add **virtue**
-To your virtue add **knowledge**
-To your knowledge add **temperance**
-To your temperance add **patience**
-To your patience add **godliness**
-To your godliness add **brotherly kindness**
-To your brotherly kindness add **charity**

If *YOU* do these things, you shall never fall (2 Peter 1:10). Remember Solomon who asked for wisdom, then added idolatry? We are the ones who add to our faith by our steady, constant, and attentive walk in the Word.

The Message Bible puts it this way:

> Everything that goes into a life of pleasing God has been miraculously given to us by getting to know, personally and intimately, the One who invited us to God. The best invitation we ever received! We were also given absolutely terrific promises to pass on to you—your tickets to participation in the life of God after you turned your back on a world corrupted by lust. So don't lose a minute in building on what you've been given, complementing your basic faith with good character, spiritual understanding, alert discipline, passionate patience, reverent wonder, warm friendliness, and generous love, each dimension fitting into and developing the others. With these qualities active and growing in your lives, no grass will grow under your feet, no day will pass without its reward as you mature in your experience of our Master Jesus.

Without these qualities you can't see what's right before you, oblivious that your old sinful life has been wiped off the books. So, friends, confirm God's invitation to you, his choice of you. Don't put it off; do it now. Do this, and you'll have your life on a firm footing, the streets paved and the way wide open into the eternal kingdom of our Master and Savior, Jesus Christ.

-2 Peter 1:3-11

Our diligence is applied most productively to the rhythm of our walk with the Lord. Colossians 3:23 tells us, "And whatsoever ye do, do it heartily, as to the Lord, and not unto men;" Solomon gave us the example of the ant in the book of Proverbs. He tells us to consider the fact that it has no overseer or ruler, and yet works on behalf of itself to make sure there is food in due season (Proverbs 6:6-8). How much more so should we, children of God, put our hands towards building the kingdom by providing spiritual food for others? We have a King who sees and knows everything, but King Jesus is not a taskmaster who demands a certain quota, He instead gives us the open-ended offer of working for Him the whole of our lives, knowing some will produce a hundredfold, some sixtyfold, and some thirtyfold (Matthew 13:8). For those who love Him, it is an honor just to be asked. Perhaps at some time or another, you have become frustrated with the call on your life. Does any of this sound familiar:

"Nobody sees me or wants to help."

"I am alone in this. The building is lonely."

"Why am I trying? What good have I accomplished?"

"I am doing all this work and not helping anyone."

Remember, God is a rewarder of those who diligently seek Him. The reward may come in waves, or it may come all at once. It may be exactly what you prayed for or it may take place long after you are gone from this world. We don't choose the reward, we simply trust in the God who gives it. Keep your focus on the big picture. Slowly, day by day, all of that hard work will have a payoff. It may be generations down the road, but your God sees you in the struggle and He is proud of you for putting your hand to the plow. He is grateful you saw Him as enough to do the work He has called you to do. If the only reward at the end is "Well done, thou good and faithful servant" then it will have all been worth it anyways.

Trust Jesus in the frustration. Nobody ever built a house to leave it empty. God is building you for a time such as this. The ants store up crumbs and call themselves blessed. Even the smallest of endeavors is equal to a mustard seed of faith in the kingdom.

Diligence in Prayer

Prayer is not a "one and done." For some issues and souls, it requires multiple prayers, perhaps even years, or decades of praying. We want miraculous healings and instant salvation, but that isn't always the case. When I begin to get frustrated with repeated prayers over the same issues, I remember God is longsuffering, and what seems like forever to me is a drop in the bucket to Him. When He is ready, He will move, until then we keep asking, seeking, and knocking, knowing that prayer is changing us and developing our hearts for seeking God and loving others.

-"Keep thy heart with all diligence; for out of it are the issues of life." Proverbs 4:23

-"Ask, and it shall be given you; seek, and ye shall find; knock, and it shall be opened unto you: For every one that asketh receiveth; and he that seeketh findeth; and to him that knocketh it shall be opened." Matthew 7:7-8

- "Let us therefore come boldly unto the throne of grace, that we may obtain mercy, and find grace to help in time of need." Hebrews 4:16

Diligence in Word

Besides salvation, the Word of God is the greatest gift given to mankind. The Lord Himself bound His heart in words and spoke them to us for spiritual food so we might taste and see that He is good. Loving God means loving His commandments and one way we show that love is to read His words as though eternity depended on them. If you are reading this book, you obviously have an interest in digging through the Word. If studying the Bible is work to you, pray that God would give you a love for His Word. Ask Him for a greater desire to read and to have a deeper understanding of what is important to Him. I believe He will gladly honor your prayer with a response and be proud of you for asking!

-"Study to shew thyself approved unto God, a workman that needeth not to be ashamed, rightly dividing the word of truth." 2 Timothy 2:15

-"Therefore shall ye lay up these my words in your heart and in your soul, and bind them for a sign upon your hand, that they may be as frontlets between your eyes. And ye shall teach them your children, speaking of them when thou sittest in thine house, and when thou walkest by the way, when thou liest down, and when thou risest up. And thou shalt write them upon the door posts of thine house, and upon thy gates:" Deuteronomy 11:18-20

-"Preach the word; be instant in season, out of season; reprove, rebuke, exhort with all long suffering and doctrine." 2 Timothy 4:2

-"And daily in the temple, and in every house, they ceased not to teach and preach Jesus Christ." Acts 5:42

Diligence in Faith

Faith can sometimes seem so hard to wrap our minds around. There is (1) the faith we have all been given to various degrees (Romans 12:3), (2) the gift of faith which is a manifestation of the Spirit (1 Corinthians 12:9), and (3) the faith we choose to have (Mark 9:23). How does one be steady, constant, and attentive in faith? By intentionally growing in it, moving in it, and abandoning the need to understand it. Little children who are growing do not sit around examining the process of their growth, they simply grow. As they grow in age, they also grow in height, maturity, experience, etc. As we walk with the Lord and grow in relationship with Him, other parts of us will grow as well. Like a child, we believe Jesus is who He says He is and can do what He says He can do.

-"And said, Verily I say unto you, Except ye be converted, and become as little children, ye shall not enter into the kingdom of heaven." Matthew 18:3

-"Verily I say unto you, Whosoever shall not receive the kingdom of God as a little child shall in no wise enter therein." Luke 18:17

-"But without faith it is impossible to please him: for he that cometh to God must believe that he is, and that he is a rewarder of them that diligently seek him." Hebrews 11:6

Diligence in Works

Our works with the Lord is the fruit of relationship, obedience, and faith. James 2:18 says, "Yea, a man may say, Thou hast faith, and I have works: shew me thy faith without thy works, and I will shew thee my faith by my works." It takes time in prayer, time in the Word, and experience to get a handle on our giftings and to find out what it looks like for us as individual followers to be productive in those gifts within the larger body of Christ. There are many ministries and many great things happening in the body, but we cannot be a part of everything, it simply isn't our job to do everything, but it is our responsibility to do what we do well. You will find abundant joy in this walk when your gifts make room for you and you begin to see Jesus' love for you as it all unfolds through the works of your hands. It is fulfilling to complete the tasks assigned to you. It may also be that you are called to create and develop new ministry opportunities for others. The possibilities are limitless because we serve a God with whom all things are possible (Matthew 19:26).

-"Whatsoever thy hand findeth to do, do it with thy might; for there is no work, nor device, nor knowledge, nor wisdom, in the grave, whither thou goest." Ecclesiastes 9:19

-"And let us not be weary in well doing: for in due season we shall reap, if we faint not." Galatians 6:9

-"Therefore, my beloved brethren, be ye stedfast, unmoveable, always abounding in the work of the Lord, forasmuch as ye know that your labour is not in vain in the Lord." 1 Corinthians 15:58

Diligence in Fellowship

Another word for fellowship is communion. There is a communion we find in the Holy Ghost, in Jesus, who is the Bread of Life. The body was always meant to be together. If you cut off your hand, you would know it! When someone is missing from fellowship, we notice. Being faithful to the church, the assembling of the body, begins with our faithfulness to the One who made us a part of the church. Without Jesus, we can do nothing. There is joy in knowing who Jesus is, being in fellowship with Him, and expressing that love to one another. Not only that, but we bear each other's burdens and encourage one another in the faith. Consistently seeking God with others is a natural part of our walk. Israel left Egypt together. The twelve apostles walked together. The Holy Ghost fell for the first time when the disciples were together. Together matters to God, so it should matter to us. There is a part of us that wants to run away sometimes and do our own thing, but obedience to the Word will always take us back to the body. After all, He is coming for one church, and we will all be lifted up together!

-"Abide in me, and I in you. As the branch cannot bear fruit of itself, except it abide in the vine; no more can ye, except ye abide in me. I am the vine, ye are the branches: He that abideth in me, and I in him, the same bringeth forth much fruit: for without me ye can do nothing." John 15:4-5

-"Not forsaking the assembling of ourselves together, as the manner of some is; but exhorting one another: and so much the more, as ye see the day approaching." Hebrews 10:25

-"For the Lord himself shall descend from heaven with a shout, with the voice of the archangel, and with the trump of God: and the dead in Christ shall rise first: Then we which are alive and remain shall be caught up together with them in the clouds, to meet the Lord in the air: and so shall we ever be with the Lord." 1 Thessalonians 4:16-17

What is the reward for diligence?

Another word for reward is "wages." Romans 6:23 tells us, "the wages of sin is death." God rewards good for good and bad for bad. For example, David tells us in his experience:

> For all his judgments were before me, and I did not put away his statutes from me. I was also upright before him, and I kept myself from mine iniquity. Therefore hath the Lord recompensed me according to my righteousness, according to the cleanness of my hands in his eyesight. With the merciful thou wilt shew thyself merciful; with an upright man thou wilt shew thyself upright;
>
> -Psalm 18:22-25

How and when God chooses to reward us is best left to Him. He knows better than anyone how to bless us:

> For God is not unrighteous to forget your work and labour of love, which ye have shewed toward his name, in that ye have ministered to the saints, and do minister. And we desire that every one of you do shew the same diligence to the full assurance of hope unto the end: That ye be not slothful, but followers of them who through faith and patience inherit the promises. For when God made promise to Abraham, because he could swear by no greater, he sware by himself, Saying, Surely blessing I will bless thee, and multiplying I will multiply thee. And so, after he had patiently endured, he obtained the promise.
>
> -Hebrews 6:10-16

Steady. Constant. Attentive- This is how we seek Jesus. Boaz told Ruth not to glean in anyone else's field (Ruth 2:8). In your building, keep your eyes on the Kingdom of Heaven. This world will offer you all the self-help you could ask for. There will be books on tips and tricks for success, but nothing will keep you in the grace of God and the will of God like the Word of God. Build your strategy around His heart and His desire for your life. There has never been anyone like you. Nobody else has ever had your unique combination of gifts and experience. Nobody else can do the work you have been chosen to do. The way we steward such an awesome call on our lives is to keep our eyes focused on the footsteps ahead of us. Those Jesus steps are intentional, purposed, ordered, and timely. There is a rhythm to our gleaning.

Steady. Constant. Attentive.

Jesus, I thank You for giving me the desire to please You and do Your work. I pray for a heart that would not grow weary in well-doing. Lord, help me to be a faithful laborer in Your field. I want to be careful with the work of my hands. I want to be someone You can trust to do Your will on earth. Help me to abound and not labor in vain. Help me to be diligent in the call which You have called me to. When it seems hard to keep going, please remind me of the bigger vision and help me endure to the end. It is in Your name I pray. Amen

"And let us not be weary in well doing: for in due season we shall reap, if we faint not." Galatians 6:9

"Therefore, my beloved brethren, be ye stedfast, unmoveable, always abounding in the work of the Lord, forasmuch as ye know that your labour is not in vain in the Lord.." 1 Corinthians 15:58

"Seest thou a man diligent in his business? he shall stand before kings; he shall not stand before mean men." Proverbs 22:29

"Wherefore the rather, brethren, give diligence to make your calling and election sure: for if ye do these things, ye shall never fall:" 2 Peter 1:10

"I press toward the mark for the prize of the high calling of God in Christ Jesus." Philippians 3:14

-How we seek Jesus matters. There is an expectation from Heaven that we will take our walk with Him seriously. We have to want to find Him!

-It takes faith to be diligent in our seeking. We must believe there is a reward at the end, even if we do not see it immediately. Jesus followers don't give up easily, they press in until they receive the blessings of God.

-The Word tells us:
> -To your faith add **virtue**
> -To your virtue add **knowledge**
> -To your knowledge add **temperance**
> -To your temperance add **patience**
> -To your patience add **godliness**
> -To your godliness add **brotherly kindness**
> -To your brotherly kindness add **charity**

-A steady, constant, and attentive pursuit of God will increase your strength and help build the kingdom. You will become more like Jesus as you grow in depth of relationship with Him.

-Wisdom is something we attain, being diligent helps us to attain God's ways. Simply by being born we have an inherent purpose to drive us towards the finish line in Christ, "what doth the Lord require of thee, but to do justly, and to love mercy, and to walk humbly with thy God?" (Micah 6:8).

PRUDENCE: COUNT THE COST

Prudence is not a word we use very much. I have never heard anyone give a compliment by saying, "I love how prudent Sally is." I have never known anyone to pray for prudence or loose it from heaven, and yet the Word tells us it is a valuable virtue.

To be prudent is to be cautious and strategic in your actions and decision-making. Much like the Proverbs 31 woman who considers her field before her purchase, one who is prudent thinks about the end results before the first move is made. Part of our definition for wisdom is having the knowledge and ability to make the right choices at the opportune time, and prudence is the application of this definition in our lives. Like a game of Jenga where the player carefully studies what will happen after the next pull, God urges us to think before we act. The act of being prudent will many times keep us from tearing down our own houses.

In real-life this might look like: not making a comment that you want to make, completing a project on time, delaying a purchase for the sake of your bank account, finishing the dishes so you won't have to deal with them in the morning, setting up a meeting to get ahead of a problem, paying off your mortgage instead of going on vacation, or fixing a hole in the fence so the cows don't get out. I could go on and on with examples and hopefully, you are thinking of some that are relevant to your life and seeing that most likely you are already operating in some form of prudence. It is a trait required in order to be a responsible adult, and even more so to be an active member of the body of Christ. Very rarely do we get to walk around doing and saying things without thinking of the consequences. To live without prudence is to walk in the flesh and be carnally minded. Mature Christians think about how their decisions affect others.

Some synonyms for prudent are: wise, sage, careful, and sensible.

The book of Proverbs tells us:

-"I wisdom dwell with prudence, and find out knowledge of witty inventions." Proverbs 8:12

-"Every prudent man dealeth with knowledge: but a fool layeth open his folly." Proverbs 13:26

-"House and riches are the inheritance of fathers: and a prudent wife is from the Lord." Proverbs 19:14

-"A prudent man foreseeth the evil, and hideth himself; but the simple pass on, and are punished." Proverbs 27:12

Count the Cost

To be prudent is to look ahead. Jesus often uses this attribute when teaching about the Kingdom of God. He doesn't want us to follow Him with a "have to" attitude, but with a "want to" attitude. He desires a people who will take up their cross and willingly go where He leads.

In the book of John, after losing many of His followers, Jesus asks the twelve if they would leave Him too. Peter's heartfelt response must have caused Jesus great joy when he said, "…

Lord, to whom shall we go? thou hast the words of eternal life" (John 6:68). Our God wants a people who have considered their options and have chosen Him over the world. This is the difference between religion and relationship. Religion is a "have to," relationship is a "want to":

> And whosoever doth not bear his cross, and come after me, cannot be my disciple. For which of you, intending to build a tower, sitteth not down first, and counteth the cost, whether he have sufficient to finish it? Lest haply, after he hath laid the foundation, and is not able to finish it, all that behold it begin to mock him, Saying, This man began to build, and was not able to finish. Or what king, going to make war against another king, sitteth not down first, and consulteth whether he be able with ten thousand to meet him that cometh against him with twenty thousand? Or else, while the other is yet a great way off, he sendeth an ambassage, and desireth conditions of peace. So likewise, whosoever he be of you that forsaketh not all that he hath, he cannot be my disciple.
>
> -Luke 14:27-33

Will you give it all to follow Jesus?

Just like a marriage, we have to come into a whole-hearted agreement that we are in it for the long run. When we decide there is no other place we would rather be than following behind Jesus, our priorities change and the life we are building becomes focused on the One who purchased our freedom. We will be all-in and sold-out for Christ. Paul said he was a "servant of Jesus Christ" (Romans 1:1). He wasn't held by bondage but instead "constrained by the love of Christ" (2 Corinthians 5:14).

Nobody knows our heart and our true motives except the Lord, so I write this paragraph as a warning and not a judgement. My concern is that in this age of Instagram and influencers, that we Christians are at risk for making our calling cheap, quick, and convenient. A post will never take the place of prayer. We are soldiers for Christ who thrive in hand-to-hand combat, meaning boots on the ground is our method for overcoming the darkness. Steward what the Lord has given you well. Social media is a highway Jesus can use; just be sure you are also doing good works in secret. When this life is over, there is only one like button that matters, "Well done, thou good and faithful servant" (Matthew 25:21).

Value

Jesus often used the idea of prudence in connection with His teaching on repentance. There is a connection between the wise use of money and the grace of God. I believe the Lord wants us to understand the true meaning of value. 1 Corinthians 6:20 tells us, "For ye are bought with a price: therefore glorify God in your body, and in your spirit, which are God's." We were not half-hazardly purchased but instead redeemed at the very high price of Jesus' blood.

Luke 15 exemplifies this idea in three parables. Each concerns value. The first parable speaks to property (sheep), the second is a lost coin (silver), and the third is relationship (son).

The Lost Sheep

"And he spake this parable unto them, saying, What man of you, having an hundred sheep, if he lose one of them, doth not leave the ninety and nine in the wilderness, and go after that which is lost, until he find it? And when he hath found it, he layeth it on his shoulders, rejoicing. And when he cometh home, he calleth together his friends and neighbours, saying unto them, Rejoice with me; for I have found my sheep which was lost. I say unto you, that likewise joy shall be in heaven over one sinner that repenteth, more than over ninety and nine just persons, which need no repentance." Luke 15:3-7

The Lost Coin

"Either what woman having ten pieces of silver, if she lose one piece, doth not light a candle, and sweep the house, and seek diligently till she find it? And when she hath found it, she calleth her friends and her neighbours together, saying, Rejoice with me; for I have found the piece which I had lost. Likewise, I say unto you, there is joy in the presence of the angels of God over one sinner that repenteth." Luke 15:8-10

The Lost Son

"And he said, A certain man had two sons: And the younger of them said to his father, Father, give me the portion of goods that falleth to me. And he divided unto them his living. And not many days after the younger son gathered all together, and took his journey into a far country, and there wasted his substance with riotous living. And when he had spent all, there arose a mighty famine in that land; and he began to be in want.

And he went and joined himself to a citizen of that country; and he sent him into his fields to feed swine. And he would fain have filled his belly with the husks that the swine did eat: and no man gave unto him. And when he came to himself, he said, How many hired servants of my father's have bread enough and to spare, and I perish with hunger! I will arise and go to my father, and will say unto him, Father, I have sinned against heaven, and before thee, And am no more worthy to be called thy son: make me as one of thy hired servants. And he arose, and came to his father. But when he was yet a great way off, his father saw him, and had compassion, and ran, and fell on his neck, and kissed him. And the son said unto him, Father, I have sinned against heaven, and in thy sight, and am no more worthy to be called thy son. But the father said to his servants, Bring forth the best robe, and put it on him; and put a ring on his hand, and shoes on his feet: And bring hither the fatted calf, and kill it; and let us eat, and be merry: For this my son was dead, and is alive again; he was lost, and is found. And they began to be merry." Luke 15:11-24

All three examples were lost, found, and celebrated. Sin happens when we don't count the cost and think ahead about the consequences of our actions- we devalue Jesus' sacrifice by moving out of the will of God. Here is the good news, however, Jesus doesn't devalue us. We become even more precious in His sight. He searches us out in our sin, remaining that steady, ever-present Father who hugs our necks and throws a party for us in our repentance.

In the book of Matthew, Jesus gives us understanding about prudence when it is used incorrectly. At the time, He was sternly warning Israel about the importance of repentance and the consequences that come when it is neglected. Jesus lifted His voice, and perhaps out of frustration, said:

> I thank thee, O Father, Lord of heaven and earth, because thou hast hid these things from the wise and prudent, and hast revealed them unto babes.
>
> -Matthew 11:25

When reading this prayer, my first thought is "What? I thought we were supposed to desire wisdom and prudence." After all, the book of Proverbs tells us they dwell together, but let us take a closer look. Just like colors come in shades, wisdom and prudence can take the form of something other than righteousness.

When wisdom and prudence are combined with wrong intention, they become guile. Synonyms for guile are crafty, cunning, and deceitful. Someone who operates in manipulation, which is a form of witchcraft, is full of guile. Basically, it is trying to get the upper hand with underhanded ways.

Jesus saw Philip of Bethsaida walking towards Him in John 1:47 and His response was an excited, "Behold an Israelite indeed, in whom is no guile!" It is safe to imagine the trait of honest intentions was a much-welcomed reprieve from all of the deception that surrounded Jesus in the temples and on the streets. In Philip's face, He saw someone who could be trusted. Someone who was doing things for the right reasons. Someone without false motives or selfish intent.

There is a verse I have on repeat in my thoughts, I keep it close as a weapon against worldly ways and selfish intent, Psalm 51:10 says, "Create in me a clean heart, O God; and renew a right spirit within me." Whenever a thought, emotion, intention, or anything else arises within me that I know is not pleasing to the Lord I say this verse over and over again until I feel it pass.

It can be tempting to try and get our way by manipulating others into how we want them to act, but this is not the will of God for us. Jesus knows the intents of our heart and He will purify us in the refining fire until all that is left is a desire to do things His way and for His purpose. We are to be kingdom-minded, not lovers of self. The world we live in promotes a life of self-indulgence. It wants you to ask yourself, "What would make me happy? How will I get noticed? How many likes, shares and follows can I get? How can I make myself the center of the world? Will a selfie do it? Will dancing on TikTok get me there?" This world wants you to believe that if you aren't viral, then you aren't acceptable. Social media is a relatively new medium and we are the generation figuring out how to give it meaning to our lives. It has given some a platform for good, but mostly it has magnified our inherent love of self. Jesus, however, has asked us to lay down our own life for the sake of others, not magnify ourselves in front of others. What we do matters. How are you answering the call on your life? Is it kingdom-minded or self-minded? Who are you putting first? Understanding how you operate in your life is a form of prudence. You aren't just flying by the seat of your pants, you are intentionally taking the back seat to elevate others. God has given you a platform, your life, as an opportunity to put others first.

Jezebel misused power and did what was evil to get her way and the consequences were big. She was full of guile, paying no regard to what was right in the eyes of the Lord. I cannot overemphasize this enough…intentions matter, and they must be submitted at the throne of grace. You and I are naturally wicked, sounds rough but it's true. Jeremiah 17:9 tells us, "The heart is deceitful above all things, and desperately wicked: who can know it?" In our natural condition, we are selfish and full of fleshly desires, but with the Word of God, the grace of God, the Holy Ghost working within us, and a fully submitted life we can war against our flesh and move in the light of Christ who "with whom is no variableness, neither shadow of turning" (James 1:17).

One Thing

Recently, I was on a trip home from a church conference when traffic slowed to a trickle. Our two lanes became one lane, and it was barely moving. There was no evidence of a wreck and nothing major seemed to have happened, but when we got far enough down the road, we saw a single truck parked on the right side which had slowed down everything. It was just one thing. One thing can make a difference. One thing can cause delay. One thing can put the main thing out of place. In the book of Revelation, Jesus warns the church of Ephesus about the importance of relationship and intentions:

> Unto the angel of the church of Ephesus write; These things saith he that holdeth the seven stars in his right hand, who walketh in the midst of the seven golden candlesticks; I know thy works, and thy labour, and thy patience, and how thou canst not bear them which are evil: and thou hast tried them which say they are apostles, and are not, and hast found them liars: And hast borne, and hast patience, and for my name's sake hast laboured, and hast not fainted. Nevertheless I have somewhat against thee, because thou hast left thy first love. Remember therefore from whence thou art fallen, and repent, and do the first works; or else I will come unto thee quickly, and will remove thy candlestick out of his place, except thou repent.
>
> -Revelation 2:1-5

Prudence is a type of spiritual common sense that keeps us looking ahead and mindful of where we are going, how we are getting there, and what we hope to achieve. If we stop paying attention and do our works on autopilot, we could end up like the church of Ephesus and almost have it right.

If you are feeling convicted now, that is a good sign that you are easily moved by the Holy Ghost. Where can you repent and start with a clean slate? Today is a good day to examine the what's, how's, and why's of this race you are running.

Philippians 2:3 tells us, "Let nothing be done through strife or vainglory; but in lowliness of mind let each esteem other better than themselves." It is so easy to get caught up in a popularity contest with the world, but we have to remember our first love and that Jesus is our reward. He is the reason we are out doing the things we are doing. It isn't for wealth or fame. If we never make a dollar, but instead only help to bring souls to salvation, then we will get to heaven thinking we have been repaid a hundredfold. Wise, sage, careful, and sensible- this is how we approach the work we are chosen for. Carefully minding to keep our eyes on the Lord who is our eternal guide.

Jesus, You said the prudent deal with knowledge, so I pray for the gift of knowledge to be poured out over my life. Lord, create in me a clean heart and renew a right spirit within me. Help the intentions of my heart be pure. I never want to do anything for vain glory, but for Your name to be glorified on the face of the earth. Keep me in Your Word so I can walk the straight and narrow path. I repent for being easily distracted by my own reputation. I submit my reputation to You. I pray for the wisdom to keep myself holy and separated. It is in Your name I pray. Amen

"Every prudent man dealeth with knowledge: but a fool layeth open his folly." Proverbs 13:16

"My little children, let us not love in word, neither in tongue; but in deed and in truth." 1 John 3:18

"Create in me a clean heart, O God; and renew a right spirit within me." Psalm 51:10

"For ye are bought with a price: therefore glorify God in your body, and in your spirit, which are God's." 1 Corinthians 6:20

-To be prudent is to be cautious and strategic about what you are doing and why you are doing it.

-Prudence and wisdom dwell together. Being a mature Christian means thinking ahead at how your actions will affect those around you.

-Jesus ties prudence to repentance by examining the relationship of value. There is value in carefully considering eternity and your actions and weighing the cost. Repentance is a time of celebration in heaven and in your heart.

-Wisdom and prudence used with the wrong intention is called guile. Guile is akin to manipulation and witchcraft. Jesus asks us to examine ourselves and submit our why's and how's to Him. Our flesh will always seek our own interest, but love is not puffed up and does not seek her own.

-We must keep our eyes on Jesus who is our first love. Relationship with Him is key to being kingdom minded. The works of our hands must be aligned with the call on our life and the reason for the call is always to win souls for heaven and to encourage the body of Christ.

DISCRETION: THE HOW MATTERS

When Jesus commanded His disciples to go forth, wisely He didn't just tell them what their assignment was, but He also told them *how* to complete it. In Matthew 10:16, Jesus warned, "Behold, I send you forth as sheep in the midst of wolves: be ye therefore wise as serpents, and harmless as doves." He reminded them about the dangers they would face in the world and to use caution when dealing with people.

Discretion is a character trait that has several meanings. We are discreet when we decide to become the keeper of valuable information. Perhaps you are aware of a sensitive conversation that could damage relationships if it were brought into the light and for the sake of discretion you keep that information to yourself. Maybe you are discreet in your actions, never behaving unseemly, but always with the right spirit and appropriate response. You may also be someone with authority who is able to make decisions at their own discretion without approval from anyone else.

Discretion is:
1. Being a good steward of private information
2. Acting in a way that is appropriate and right
3. Having authority to make decision

The thread that holds the meaning of the word discretion together is the element of *how*. Just as a ballerina moves differently than a tap dancer, a discreet person moves differently than a hasty person. There are circumstances that call for quick decisions, but more times than not we should glide across our life with discretion and not buffalo our way through one decision at a time.

When we work with a discreet spirit, we are building our house carefully and with authority.

The book of Proverbs tells us:

- "The proverbs of Solomon the son of David, king of Israel...To give subtilty to the simple, to the young man knowledge and discretion." Proverbs 1:1-4

-"Discretion shall preserve thee, understanding shall keep thee:" Proverbs 2:11

-"My son, let not them depart from thine eyes: keep sound wisdom and discretion: So shall they be life unto thy soul, and grace to thy neck." Proverbs 3:21-22

-"My son, attend unto my wisdom, and bow thine ear to my understanding: That thou mayest regard discretion, and that thy lips may keep knowledge." Proverbs 5:1-2

-"As a jewel of gold in a swine's snout, so is a fair woman which is without discretion." Proverbs 11:22

-"The discretion of a man deferreth his anger; and it is his glory to pass over a transgression." Proverbs 19:11

Since we know the works of our hands are made fruitful by our relationship with Jesus, we must ask ourselves, "How am I moving out of my relationship? Are my days carefully gliding across the pages of my life?"

After the Spirit led Jesus into the wilderness and He fasted for forty days, Satan came to Him with options (Matthew 4:1-11). He wanted Jesus to make quick decisions that would alter the way things were going. He wanted to know how Jesus would move:

1. Will you move from a place of hunger?
   "And when the tempter came to him, he said, If thou be the Son of God, command that these stones be made bread." Matthew 4:1-3
2. Will you move from a lack of knowledge?
   "Then the devil taketh him up into the holy city, and setteth him on a pinnacle of the temple, And saith unto him, If thou be the Son of God, cast thyself down: for it is written, He shall give his angels charge concerning thee: and in their hands they shall bear thee up, lest at any time thou dash thy foot against a stone." Matthew 4:5-6
3. Will you move from greed?
   "Again, the devil taketh him up into an exceeding high mountain, and sheweth him all the kingdoms of the world, and the glory of them; And saith unto him, All these things will I give thee, if thou wilt fall down and worship me." Matthew 4:8-9

With every test the enemy threw His way, Jesus carefully responded with the Word of God. He wielded the Word like an expert craftsman, not half-hazardly, but with precision, cutting down the imagined authority of the enemy who was using the Word with bad form and bad intent. Every time Satan came at Him, He answered with an "It is written…" Jesus proved the way He moves is with wise discretion:

1. I move from the Word of God…
    "But he answered and said, It is written, Man shall not live by bread alone, but by every word that proceedeth out of the mouth of God." Matthew 4:4
2. I move with understanding…
    "Jesus said unto him, It is written again, Thou shalt not tempt the Lord thy God." Matthew 4:7
3. I move with devotion…
    "Then saith Jesus unto him, Get thee hence, Satan: for it is written, Thou shalt worship the Lord thy God, and him only shalt thou serve." Matthew 4:10

The Crooked Manager

Jesus gives us an awkward parable in the book of Luke. Very much like His directions to be wise as a serpent, we might read this parable of the crooked manager and wonder if Jesus really meant to tell us this one. After all, it has a bit of a twist to it. The Message version tells it to us like this:

> Jesus said to his disciples, "There was once a rich man who had a manager. He got reports that the manager had been taking advantage of his position by running up huge personal

expenses. So he called him in and said, 'What's this I hear about you? You're fired. And I want a complete audit of your books.' "The manager said to himself, 'What am I going to do? I've lost my job as manager. I'm not strong enough for a laboring job, and I'm too proud to beg. . . . Ah, I've got a plan. Here's what I'll do . . . then when I'm turned out into the street, people will take me into their houses.' "Then he went at it. One after another, he called in the people who were in debt to his master. He said to the first, 'How much do you owe my master?' "He replied, 'A hundred jugs of olive oil.' "The manager said, 'Here, take your bill, sit down here—quick now—write fifty.' "To the next he said, 'And you, what do you owe?' "He answered, 'A hundred sacks of wheat.' "He said, 'Take your bill, write in eighty.' "Now here's a surprise: The master praised the crooked manager! And why? Because he knew how to look after himself. Streetwise people are smarter in this regard than law-abiding citizens. They are on constant alert, looking for angles, surviving by their wits. I want you to be smart in the same way—but for what is right— using every adversity to stimulate you to creative survival, to concentrate your attention on the bare essentials, so you'll live, really live, and not complacently just get by on good behavior."

-Luke 16:1-9

This parable shows a side of Jesus that I find really interesting. This is the side of Jesus that turns tables over and curses fig trees. This is the scrappy side that makes Him unpredictable and fascinating. Here Jesus is saying, "I want more than your perfect behavior. I want you to be all in. I want you to care about the outcome. I want you to use your mind and be creative. I want you to not only survive this world but to thrive in a way that is surprising and real." This is the side of Jesus that picks fishermen and misfits to set the world on fire.

Stewardship matters to God. It isn't just about what we are given, it is also *how* we manage it. In the parable of the crooked manager, Jesus wasn't applauding the fraud, he was applauding the wit the manager used to get himself off the streets. He used what time he had to better his situation by thinking outside the box. This is how we are supposed to think- outside the box! Imagine how quickly we can get people into the kingdom by partnering with the Holy Ghost to develop creative outlets for His Spirit to flow in ministry. God wants to do something through you that He has never done before. You are a new creature in Christ, and the work He does through you is new. New to the world. New to the kingdom. New to you! In this parable, Jesus is giving us permission to look for the advantage. He wants us to discreetly use our minds and our gifts to get the best this world has to offer. Take a look at the gifts you have been given and ask yourself how you can use them in a way others haven't thought of before. We are a people who like to invent. The paper these words were written on, the ink they were printed with, the font of the letters, and the computer on which it was written- someone had to develop all of this. Someone had to take it from idea to conception and now here we are using these inventions for the Kingdom of God. Maybe your contribution to the kingdom isn't so obvious as a preacher or teacher, but instead of seeing that as a frustration, look at it as a treasure hunt. Your gift has been discreetly hidden within you by the Creator of the Universe so that you can have the opportunity to discover and explore the new things you will bring to His table. My mother has a ring with all of her kid's birthstones on them. If you didn't know the story behind the ring you would think it was a collection of random jewels, but once I tell you how each jewel fits together, then the whole piece makes sense. The ring is even more beautiful because of the meaning behind *how* the jewels were chosen. Your gifts are this way, too. They may seem random at first, but when God reveals to you piece by piece the meaning and purpose behind each one, the story of YOU will be so beautiful you will be glad it took time for you to unearth it all.

Hopefully, you are feeling inspired to find out more about what God has gifted you, but I would like to add a warning- You have opposition. There is a thief who would like nothing better than to stop you in your tracks. This is why we have to be a little scrappy ourselves. If it's a fight the devil is after, we will be the ones to give it to him. In the book of Acts, Luke tells an interesting story about Paul and an experience he had as a new preacher (9:25). The early days of his preaching were getting him in trouble with the Jews and when the plot to kill him was found out, his new friends the disciples helped him escape by lowering him out of the window in a basket. The disciples knew how to think outside the box!

My family and I have two cats. May, our inside cat, lays around, eats, and cries for treats every time we come in. She is a fluffy, spoiled, much-loved house cat and she knows it. May had it pretty easy until Winston, our Yorkie, came along. Winston seems to think he and May are in a perpetual football game. He loves to chase her, pounce on her, and run her into a corner. Poor May doesn't put up much of a fight either. Usually, when this happens, she waves her precious paw a few times in his direction and waits to be rescued. Our outside cat, Pumpkin, however, is a whole different story. Don't let the name fool you, Pumpkin is a fighter, a street cat. It only took Winston a few days to learn he doesn't want the wrong end of Pumpkin. Guess which cat he devotes his attention to? Guess which cat he runs from? We have to be a little more like Pumpkin and a little less like May. Discretion doesn't mean we sit by and let the Devil have his way. Discretion means we outwit the enemy. We are strategic in our prayer life, thoughtful in our approach, and we wield the Word like an expert craftsman, speaking truth and resisting the devil who is out to steal, kill, and destroy.

-"And from the days of John the Baptist until now the kingdom of heaven suffereth violence, and the violent take it by force." Matthew 11:12

-"Thou therefore endure hardness, as a good soldier of Jesus Christ." 2 Timothy 2:3

-"Behold, I come quickly: hold that fast which thou hast, that no man take thy crown." Revelation 3:11

Jesus, I thank you for teaching me not just what to do, but for also teaching me the how and why. I want to guide my affairs with discretion. I want to be someone You trust with Your biggest secrets and hardest cases. Help me to be humble so that I am not easily offended. I know Your ways are not my ways, and I would much rather do things the way You do them. Give me ears to hear so I don't miss a thing. Please redeem situations and relationships where I moved incorrectly. Mend broken fences and hurt feelings. It is in Your name I pray. Amen

"A good man sheweth favour, and lendeth: he will guide his affairs with discretion." Psalm 112:5

"The discretion of a man deferreth his anger; and it is his glory to pass over a transgression..." Proverbs 19:11

"Listen to me now. Give me your closest attention. Do farmers plow and plow and do nothing but plow? Or harrow and harrow and do nothing but harrow? After they've prepared the ground, don't they plant? Don't they scatter dill and spread cumin, Plant wheat and barley in the fields and raspberries along the borders? They know exactly what to do and when to do it. Their God is their teacher. And at the harvest, the delicate herbs and spices, the dill and cumin, are treated delicately. On the other hand, wheat is threshed and milled, but still not endlessly. The farmer knows how to treat each kind of grain. He's learned it all from God-of-the-Angel-Armies, who knows everything about when and how and where." Isaiah 28:23-29 *The Message*

- The how matters! Jesus cares as much about how we do something as He does what we are doing.

-Discretion is about the how. How do you handle sensitive information? How do you use authority? How do you conduct business? We have to be a people who move wisely, appropriately, and thoughtfully.

-In the wilderness, Jesus was tempted with quick fixes. Satan mishandled the Word to try and pressure Jesus into messing up the plan. Jesus, however, thoughtfully wielded the Word with power and turned the tables over on the enemy. You can do the same thing!

-God rewards creative stewardship. You have a unique combination of gifts that make your story with Jesus more exciting and more beautiful. He has made your life a treasure hunt and wants you to enjoy the process of discovery.

-The enemy wants to keep you on the sidelines and steal your purpose. Jesus followers have permission to be a little scrappy for the kingdom- not in a way that is sinful, but in a way that is wise like a serpent and innocent like a dove- that takes some imagination!

KNOWLEDGE: THE BRIDGE

Throughout the book of Proverbs, we learn to be intentional with our lives and our interests. We can't simply go with the flow of the world, but instead as mature Christians, we partner with the Holy Ghost who steers and directs our individual lives toward an end goal. How many days and nights have you spent trying to figure out the end goal? Isn't it easier to team up with the One who made you and seek His knowledge of who you are and where you are going? I would argue the chief pursuit of mankind has been spent trying to figure out what is next and how to get there. Relationship with Jesus means trusting Him for the end result, "For I know the thoughts that I think toward you, saith the Lord, thoughts of peace, and not of evil, to give you an expected end" (Jeremiah 29:11).

One of the key differences between a leader and a follower is that a leader wants to direct the ship while a follower wants to be directed. The leader, however, is simply just serving the follower's needs. Everyone is leading someone and everyone is following someone. As Jesus followers we all follow in His footsteps.

It is good to sit with the Lord and find out how you are built. Personality, giftings, and how willing you are to submit your life plays a pivotal role in where you are headed. Has Jesus called you to direct the flow or has He called you to work on the ship? Both are good and both are necessary. Most likely it is a combination of the two. There will be areas of your life where you call the shots and areas where you obey the wisdom of Ephesians 5:21, operating under the authority of others,

"Submitting yourselves one to another in the fear of God." After all, what truly matters is who you are serving while you do what you are doing.

Regardless of your call, knowledge is something we all need to do our jobs well. Knowledge is the bridge between where we are and what comes next. Without it we are stagnant in the water, not moving forward, not really going backward, just stuck where we are searching the horizon for a way to advance.

Knowledge is:
1. What is true
2. The ability to work with what is true

What you have been called to do for the kingdom is like a cake with many ingredients. The life God has chosen you for is viable based on His character and ability combined with your character and ability in Him. Knowing things is so much a part of who Jesus is, that we too must have a mind and desire to know who He is, what He has called us for, the information pertaining to that call, and the ability to use our knowledge to achieve the expected end.

The book of Proverbs tells us:

-"A wise man will hear, and will increase learning; and a man of understanding shall attain unto wise counsels:" Proverbs 1:5

-"The fear of the Lord is the beginning of knowledge: but fools despise wisdom and instruction." Proverbs 1:7

-"When wisdom entereth into thine heart, and knowledge is pleasant unto thy soul; Discretion shall preserve thee, understanding shall keep thee:" Proverbs 2:10-11

-"The Lord by wisdom hath founded the earth; by understanding hath he established the heavens. By his knowledge the depths are broken up, and the clouds drop down the dew." Proverbs 3:19-20

-"The fear of the Lord is the beginning of wisdom: and the knowledge of the holy is understanding. For by me thy days shall be multiplied, and the years of thy life shall be increased." Proverbs 9:10-11

-"The heart of him that hath understanding seeketh knowledge: but the mouth of fools feedeth on foolishness." Proverbs 15:14

-"The heart of the prudent getteth knowledge; and the ear of the wise seeketh knowledge." Proverbs 18:15

-"A wise man is strong; yea, a man of knowledge increaseth strength." Proverbs 24:5

We can gather from these scriptures that wise and strong members of the body of Christ seek knowledge, but the foolish want nothing to do with knowledge, instead choosing to enjoy foolishness.

There is another category of knowledge seekers we learn about from Jesus in the book of Luke. When talking to the lawyers,

He admonished them by saying, "Woe unto you, lawyers! for ye have taken away the key of knowledge: ye entered not in yourselves, and them that were entering in ye hindered" (11:52). How I translate this in my way of speaking is, "You know what the right thing is, but you aren't living it and you aren't teaching it either." In other words, there is a key to knowledge but just sitting on knowledge and not doing anything with it does nobody any good. God calls us to be doers and not just hearers (James 1:22).

This might be the key to your calling…

-What knowledge has God given you access to that will help others?
-How can you use that knowledge to encourage the body of believers?
-Where does it lead you that you might encounter a lost soul in need of the saving grace of Jesus Christ?

When God changed Saul to Paul and redirected his life into the ministry, He didn't wipe clean his memory bank or his past experiences. He called Paul into ministry and gave him a new life that built upon who he already was. There were parts of him that were good and useful to the building of Christianity throughout the world. His zeal and his passion for doing what was right didn't change, what changed was Paul's understanding of what was right. In Philippians 3:8 he writes, "Yea doubtless, and I count all things but loss for the excellency of the knowledge of Christ Jesus my Lord: for whom I have suffered the loss of all things, and do count them but dung, that I may win Christ," From this, we can gather that the most important information we will ever have is Christ and Him crucified. Every piece of knowledge we possess in our life stems from the truth of the gospel…who Jesus is and what He did for us.

The Anointing Will Teach You

You are chosen to build, and God wants you to be a successful builder. There is an anointing on your life to break yokes. How do you know what and how to build? The Word tells us:

> But the anointing which ye have received of him abideth in you, and ye need not that any man teach you: but as the same anointing teacheth you of all things, and is truth, and is no lie, and even as it hath taught you, ye shall abide in him.
>
> -1 John 2:27

When we abide (live in, dwell in, make our home in) Jesus, He will take charge of our education. You will be taught through the power of the Holy Ghost. You will be driven to the Word, driven to prayer, driven to the right influences, and driven to church. The drive to learn more about who Jesus is and how to be excellent in your call will keep you. Now, there will be days when your flesh wants to take over. Days when you want to watch Netflix instead of praying and stay at home instead of going to church, but you will gird yourself in truth and go despite your flesh. You will keep your eyes on the One who called you and ignore the voice of the enemy because you know there is a bigger picture at stake.

There are times when we need specific information that only God can give to us and because He is good to His children, He simply gives it to us freely. For me, this often comes at night when I am quiet and still. Jesus will often teach you about your calling by waking you up and allowing you to experience it within your imagination and through your spirit. This is why we must submit our imagination to Him, so He can have free access to guide us into His truth for our future:

> Nevertheless, I tell you the truth; It is expedient for you that I go away: for if I go not away, the Comforter will not come unto you; but if I depart, I will send him unto you…Howbeit when he, the Spirit of truth, is come, he will guide you into all truth: for he shall not speak of himself; but whatsoever he shall hear, that shall he speak: and he will shew you things to come.
>
> -John 16:7-13

The experiences you have in the Holy Ghost are not separate from Jesus, they are Jesus. He is the Holy Ghost. Jesus is still calling and directing lives for His purpose. He is intimately concerned with His beloved, the ones He has called to serve Him and advance the kingdom. You should be seeking out this one-on-one relationship with Jesus and asking Him to speak to you personally about how you will serve. He wants to spend that time with you and be that important to you. He delights in you.

There is a gift of knowledge that comes through the Spirit. It can't be taught by man. It can't be bought through more schooling. It can't be received any other way than through the Spirit of God releasing information into your heart and mind:

> Now there are diversities of gifts, but the same Spirit. And there are differences of administrations, but the same Lord. And there are diversities of operations, but it is the same God which worketh all in all. But the manifestation of the Spirit is given to every man to profit withal. For to one is given by the Spirit the word of wisdom; to another the word of knowledge by the same Spirit; To another faith by the same Spirit; to another the gifts of healing by the same Spirit; To another the working of miracles; to another prophecy; to another discerning of spirits; to another divers kinds of tongues; to another the interpretation of tongues: But all these worketh that one and the selfsame Spirit, dividing to every man severally as he will. For as the body is one, and hath many members, and all the members of that one body, being many, are one body: so also is Christ.
>
> -1 Corinthians 12:4-12

The gift of knowledge will edify the body of Christ. Knowing things beyond what we should know in the natural is not for our own self-satisfaction but is always to be of service to someone else or to keep us in the way we should go. For example, God may give you knowledge of someone's pain so you can minister to that person. Perhaps, Jesus will talk to you and give you a strategy, so you know how to move in a certain situation. Perhaps you will know the exact right thing to say at the exact right time. This gift may come across as very practical, but it is always supernatural- something you would not know if the Lord had not given you the information.

God will send the right person at the right time…

I have a friend who once said she didn't care how God gave her information as long as He gave it to her. When we are seeking out knowledge it can come in all manner of forms. The book of Acts tells us about Cornelius who had been praying always when an angel came and gave him specific instructions on how to get more information about God:

> A devout man, and one that feared God with all his house, which gave much alms to the people, and prayed to God alway. He saw in a vision evidently about the ninth hour of the day an angel of God coming in to him, and saying unto him, Cornelius. And when he looked on him, he was afraid, and said, What is it, Lord? And he said unto him, Thy prayers and thine alms are come up for a memorial before God. And now send men to Joppa, and call for one Simon, whose surname is Peter: He lodgeth with one Simon a tanner, whose house is by the sea side: he shall tell thee what thou oughtest to do. And when the angel which spake unto

Cornelius was departed, he called two of his household servants, and a devout soldier of them that waited on him continually;

-Acts 10:2-7

I'm not sure how many times in our lives an angel will be sent to give us directions on where to find our answers, but I do believe God always answers our fervent prayers and desires to know Him better. While this angel was instructing Cornelius, Peter was on a rooftop having a vision that would unlock his understanding of what would come. This is how God works. He prepares everyone for the big reveal. Cornelius was being instructed by the angel. Peter was given the vision. When the two got together Cornelius' desire fit perfectly with Peter's revelation and the beautiful outcome was beyond expectation:

> While Peter yet spake these words, the Holy Ghost fell on all them which heard the word. And they of the circumcision which believed were astonished, as many as came with Peter, because that on the Gentiles also was poured out the gift of the Holy Ghost. For they heard them speak with tongues, and magnify God. Then answered Peter, Can any man forbid water, that these should not be baptized, which have received the Holy Ghost as well as we? And he commanded them to be baptized in the name of the Lord. Then prayed they him to tarry certain days.

-Acts 10:44-48

I have the sweetest mother in the world and one day she was leaving her house to go to a women's conference down the road when she saw a car pulled over to the side. Two well-dressed women were standing by a red Honda looking at their phones. My mom drove past them when it dawned on her that they were probably lost on their way to the very same conference as her. She turned around, pulled over, and asked the confused women where they were headed. Indeed, they were lost, and were trying to get to the same place, when she offered to guide them, one of the ladies spoke up and said, "I've been praying for you."

Cornelius had a need and Peter was the answer.
Peter had a calling and Cornelius was the key.

This moment in time was a revelation played out that would bring redemption to the Gentiles and show Peter that God is no respecter of persons. God will send the right person at the right time.

Overcoming Grasshopper Mentality

After the Israelites had wandered in the wilderness, God told Moses to send a troop to scout out the land of Canaan and report back. Moses chose the explorers and told him he wanted information on who was there, what they were like, and what they could expect before they entered the promise. This group searched out the land for forty days and when they came back, they had plenty to say. God had indeed given them a land flowing with milk and honey. It was wonderful. There were fruits and fields. Everything they desired and were told they could have, only there was a problem…the Israelites had a grasshopper mentality. They could see the good, but the effort to have it was more than their confidence could handle:

> Nevertheless the people be strong that dwell in the land, and the cities are walled, and very great: and moreover we saw the children of Anak there…And there we saw the giants, the sons of Anak, which come of the giants: and we were in our own sight as grasshoppers, and so we were in their sight.
>
> -Numbers 13:28-33

The Israelites suffered from a defeated spirit. They counted themselves as down and out before the battle even started. They forgot they had the advantage. God was for them. God was on their side. God would fight for them. The knowledge of the land and the challenges they faced became bigger in their sight than the knowledge that the Lord directed their path. The Israelites scouted the land in Numbers but received the promise in Exodus:

> And I have said, I will bring you up out of the affliction of Egypt unto the land of the Canaanites, and the Hittites, and the Amorites, and the Perizzites, and the Hivites, and the Jebusites, unto a land flowing with milk and honey.
>
> -Exodus 3:17

Caleb had a different spirit of course. Caleb said, "Let us go up at once, and possess it; for we are well able to overcome it" (Numbers 13:30). Caleb hadn't forgotten about the Lord.

Whatever you are called to do will take a different spirit. There will be obstacles and battles standing in-between where you are and where you are called to be.

Don't let the knowledge of the battle overshadow the knowledge of Jesus, who He is and what He does. Let your relationship with Him be the catalyst and confidence you need to overcome giants.

Jesus, I thank you for gifting knowledge to Your people. Lord, I depend on You to see me through the situations I don't know how to handle. I depend on You to guide me into all truth. Let Your Spirit be manifested in my life through the word of knowledge. Let my relationship with You be like a city on a hill that cannot be hidden. I want to build from Your blueprints, because I see that it is only through You that others are truly helped. Manmade ways of doing things will never work. I pray for divine inspiration for every move I make. It is in Your name I pray. Amen

"The fear of the Lord is the beginning of knowledge: but fools despise wisdom and instruction." Proverbs 1:7

"My people are destroyed for lack of knowledge: because thou hast rejected knowledge, I will also reject thee, that thou shalt be no priest to me: seeing thou hast forgotten the law of thy God, I will also forget thy children." Hosea 4:6

"But the manifestation of the Spirit is given to every man to profit withal. For to one is given by the Spirit the word of wisdom; to another the word of knowledge by the same Spirit; To another faith by the same Spirit; to another the gifts of healing by the same Spirit; To another the working of miracles; to another prophecy; to another discerning of spirits; to another divers kinds of tongues; to another the interpretation of tongues: But all these worketh that one and the selfsame Spirit, dividing to every man severally as he will." 1 Corinthians 12:7-11

-Relationship with Jesus means trusting Him to give us what we need to accomplish the calling on our lives.

-Knowledge is the bridge between where we are and what comes next. Without it we are stagnant in the water, not moving forward, not really going backward, just stuck where we are searching the horizon for a way to advance.

-The Holy Ghost will guide us into truth. Our knowledge of Jesus through the Word is the source of all knowledge. Sometimes, however, the Lord downloads information we need into our spirit, the gift of knowledge is a supernatural way of receiving information, and sometimes He sends the right person at the right time. It doesn't matter how we get the information, so long as we get it!

-There is a heavenly solution to every problem. God has a plan for your breakthrough. Revelation is waiting to direct you into the next step.

-The Israelites let the knowledge of their obstacles take precedence over the promises of God over their life. They saw themselves in relation to circumstance, not in relation to what God had told them about their future. Obtaining the promise means choosing what information will the biggest motivator in your life.

FAVOR: WITH GOD AND MAN

In the book of Luke, after Jesus' parents found Him teaching in the temple, we are told He submitted to them. The next verse says, "And Jesus increased in wisdom and stature, and in favour with God and man" (Luke 2:52). We learn from this verse that favor is something that can increase in our life and happens only in a life of submission. Submission to God and authority. We seek favor because it opens doors of opportunity and expands our influence. We seek opportunity and influence because it expands the Kingdom of God and gives Him glory.

We are chosen to build in relationship with Jesus. He is the source of our favor. Another way of explaining favor is the amount of grace on your life to achieve what God has purposed for you. When we think of favor in a worldly way we think of big visible blessings- wealth, position, health, and other high-minded signs that the Lord is on your side. The thing about favor, however, is that for the one who bears the favor it often doesn't feel that way.

David ran from Saul…still favored.
Joseph was thrown in a pit…still favored.
Stephen was stoned to death…still favored.
Paul was imprisoned…still favored.
Jesus was hung on a cross…still favored.

We can look back on these examples and see the obvious hand of God and purpose of God on their lives, but at the moment Jesus was hung on the cross even He asked why He had been forsaken. Because favor doesn't always feel like a blessing, it has to be rehearsed and meditated on in our minds and our inner man. I'm sure when David was running he reminded himself about being anointed in the field, when Joseph was in prison he drew strength from the dreams he had years ago, when Stephen was stoned he looked up to heaven, when Paul was imprisoned he remembered the road to Damascus, and when Jesus was hung on the cross He honored His commitment in the Garden of Gethsemane.

The book of Proverbs tells us:

-"My son, forget not my law; but let thine heart keep my commandments: For length of days, and long life, and peace, shall they add to thee. Let not mercy and truth forsake thee: bind them about thy neck; write them upon the table of thine heart: So shalt thou find favour and good understanding in the sight of God and man." Proverbs 3:1-4

-"The curse of the Lord is in the house of the wicked: but he blesseth the habitation of the just. Surely he scorneth the scorners: but he giveth grace unto the lowly. The wise shall inherit glory: but shame shall be the promotion of fools." Proverbs 3:33-35

Favor is a great thing so long as it is used to promote the kingdom. There are a lot of people in the world with favor, for example, actors and musicians get a red carpet rolled out for them at fancy events. They are photographed and applauded. The entertainment industry is full of worldly favor (special treatment that is bought through talent and wealth). This favor, however, is deceitful. It comes and goes based on opinions and bank accounts. An actor makes a bad movie…poof…they lost their favor. A musician makes an album nobody wants to listen to…boom…everything they thought they had is gone. What you are building needs firm foundations.

I once had a dream that I was building a hotel. I built it floor after floor until it was so high I had to look up at it from the ground. Opening the door, I invited everyone I could find inside to stay and enjoy this tower that was built. Suddenly, the foundations started to shake and I realized the whole thing would collapse because I didn't take time to build the right footing. Foundations matter. Making decisions based on man-pleasing is not a true set of directions from which to build.

What God is doing in you and through you needs the favor that comes from being pleasing to the Lord and doing His will.

The flip side to favor is the warning found in Proverbs 31:30, "Favour is deceitful, and beauty is vain: but a woman that feareth the Lord, she shall be praised." Worldly favor and Godly favor are two different manifestations. We can see the friction between the two in the story of Ballam and Balak in the book of Numbers 22:1-24:25.

Balak was a king of Moab who sought out Ballam to curse the Israelites. The king wanted to pay him with his worldly favor, however, God had another plan for Israel. The Lord would use Balak's own plot against him and the prophet who the king beckoned to curse would be the mouthpiece of blessing. Three times Balam blessed Israel in front of the king and three times the king grew angry. What Balak didn't understand was the favor that Israel had to be blessed and not cursed. They were God's chosen people living in covenant with the One who delivered them from Egypt. The Lord wasn't going to just sit by and watch as they were cursed. He had a plan for their salvation. He had a plan of rescue. The king wanted to pay the prophet with his favor but the prophet could not move beyond the word of God over Israel and the favor that rested on them. From this exchange we learn a fundamental truth about God's nature and the strength of His promises, Numbers 23:19 tells us, "God is not a man, that he should lie; neither the son of man, that he should repent: hath he said, and shall he not do it? or hath he spoken, and shall he not make it good?"

The words God speaks over you are an indicator of the grace He has given you to move into the areas you are called to build. How do you hear these words? For many it is prayer and quiet time with the Lord. He will talk to you and guide you into the knowledge of the call, blessing you as you walk with Him in the process of your building. You may experience a prophetic word spoken over you by someone operating the gift of prophecy. The gift of prophecy is a manifestation of the Spirit in which God uses to edify His church and draw in the unbeliever:

> But if all prophesy, and there come in one that believeth not, or one unlearned, he is convinced of all, he is judged of all: And thus are the secrets of his heart made manifest; and so falling down on his face he will worship God, and report that God is in you of a truth.
>
> -1 Corinthians 14:24-25

If you haven't had a prophetic word spoken over you, there are a multitude of promises in the Bible you can speak over yourself in prayer to promote favor and rehearse your covenant with Jesus.

For example:

-"What shall we then say to these things? If God be for us, who can be against us? He that spared not his own Son, but delivered him up for us all, how shall he not with him also freely give us all things? Who shall lay any thing to the charge of God's elect? It is God that justifieth." Romans 8:31-33

-"The blessing of the Lord, it maketh rich, and he addeth no sorrow with it." Proverbs 10:22

-"In that I command thee this day to love the Lord thy God, to walk in his ways, and to keep his commandments and his statutes and his judgments, that thou mayest live and multiply: and the Lord thy God shall bless thee in the land whither thou goest to possess it." Deuteronomy 30:16

-"And the Lord shall deliver me from every evil work, and will preserve me unto his heavenly kingdom: to whom be glory for ever and ever. Amen." 2 Timothy 4:18

Some of the greatest promises of God come from a life of obedience to the Lord. Favor on our lives is simply a result from knowing God's will and doing it wholeheartedly:

> And it shall come to pass, if thou shalt hearken
> diligently unto the voice of the Lord thy God,
> to observe and to do all his commandments

which I command thee this day, that the Lord thy God will set thee on high above all nations of the earth: and all these blessings shall come on thee, and overtake thee, if thou shalt hearken unto the voice of the Lord thy God. Blessed shalt thou be in the city, and blessed shalt thou be in the field. Blessed shall be the fruit of thy body, and the fruit of thy ground, and the fruit of thy cattle, the increase of thy kine, and the flocks of thy sheep. Blessed shall be thy basket and thy store. Blessed shalt thou be when thou comest in, and blessed shalt thou be when thou goest out. The Lord shall cause thine enemies that rise up against thee to be smitten before thy face: they shall come out against thee one way, and flee before thee seven ways. The Lord shall command the blessing upon thee in thy storehouses, and in all that thou settest thine hand unto; and he shall bless thee in the land which the Lord thy God giveth thee. The Lord shall establish thee an holy people unto himself, as he hath sworn unto thee, if thou shalt keep the commandments of the Lord thy God, and walk in his ways. And all people of the earth shall see that thou art called by the name of the Lord; and they shall be afraid of thee. And the Lord shall make thee plenteous in goods, in the fruit of thy body, and in the fruit of thy cattle, and in the fruit of thy ground, in the land which the Lord sware unto thy fathers to give thee. The

Lord shall open unto thee his good treasure, the heaven to give the rain unto thy land in his season, and to bless all the work of thine hand: and thou shalt lend unto many nations, and thou shalt not borrow. And the Lord shall make thee the head, and not the tail; and thou shalt be above only, and thou shalt not be beneath; if that thou hearken unto the commandments of the Lord thy God, which I command thee this day, to observe and to do them: and thou shalt not go aside from any of the words which I command thee this day, to the right hand, or to the left, to go after other gods to serve them.

-Deuteronomy 28:1-14

In this passage from Deuteronomy, God promises:

-He will set us high above all nations of the earth
-Blessings wherever we go
-All our fruit and land will be blessed
-Increase and plenty
-Our enemies will be smitten
-We will be established

What a blessing of favor! This all belongs to the child of God who follows the Word and the will of God for their lives. It almost seems too good to be true, except it is…this is the God we serve. The God for whom nothing is impossible. The God who gives good gifts to His children. The God who cares about the outcome. The God who keeps His promises.

When Moses encountered God in the burning bush, part of the promise of his commission to help lead the Israelites out of bondage was wrapped in favor. The Lord told Moses, "And I will give this people favour in the sight of the Egyptians: and it shall come to pass, that, when ye go, ye shall not go empty" (Exodus 3:21).

This is the God we serve. The God who never sends us out empty.

A Warning About Favor

There is a warning, however, that continues in the story of Israel after they received the blessings from Balaam. We ended it earlier with Israel coming out ahead against the King of the Moabs in Numbers 24. The very next chapter begins this way: "And Israel abode in Shittim, and the people began to commit whoredom with the daughters of Moab" (Numbers 25:1).

What a disappointment. God went through all that effort to bless them and keep them from the curses of Balak and yet the Israelites reversed their blessings by disobeying God's command to keep themselves separate. This act of rebellion against His Word kindled the anger of the Lord. He was not happy. God caused a plague to come and twenty-four thousand people died. This, my friend, is the fear of the Lord. We serve a mighty God who is able to make anything come to pass. Gratefully, we are on this side the cross and when we misalign ourselves outside of His will, we can repent, turn away from the sin, and be forgiven. Their disobedient example, however, is still a good reminder that being blessed one day does not mean you can turn from the Word of God. King Saul lost favor when he disobeyed God (1 Samuel 15:1-35). He did most of what was told to him, but not all. Living our lives in His will and in His way is the key to open doors, follow the command to study and show yourself approved, then do what it is the Spirit of the Lord is telling you to do (2 Timothy 2:15).

The Beauty of Favor

The Song of Solomon is a beautiful book detailing the deep, passionate love between the Shulamite and her Beloved. This book signifies the relationship between Jesus and His church, and because we are the church, it gives us a deeper understanding of our individual relationship with Jesus. We worship a God who gives us favor not simply because we are obedient, but also because we are greatly loved. Just like the love between a husband and wife, this is a love that grows and deepens over time.

1. Jesus' love for us makes us feel special. It is close and designed to be an intimate experience between you and the God who cherishes you:

   "I am the rose of Sharon, and the lily of the valleys. As the lily among thorns, so is my love among the daughters. As the apple tree among the trees of the wood, so is my beloved among the sons. I sat down under his shadow with great delight, and his fruit was sweet to my taste. He brought me to the banqueting house, and his banner over me was love. Stay me with flagons, comfort me with apples: for I am sick of love. His left hand is under my head, and his right hand doth embrace me." Song of Solomon 2:1-6

2. The favor of the Lord on our lives moves us into beautiful new seasons. There is always something new on the horizon, a hope to look forward to.

    "My beloved spake, and said unto me, Rise up, my love, my fair one, and come away. For, lo, the winter is past, the rain is over and gone; The flowers appear on the earth; the time of the singing of birds is come, and the voice of the turtle is heard in our land; The fig tree putteth forth her green figs, and the vines with the tender grape give a good smell. Arise, my love, my fair one, and come away. O my dove, that art in the clefts of the rock, in the secret places of the stairs, let me see thy countenance, let me hear thy voice; for sweet is thy voice, and thy countenance is comely. Take us the foxes, the little foxes, that spoil the vines: for our vines have tender grapes. My beloved is mine, and I am his: he feedeth among the lilies." Song of Solomon 2:10-16

3. Our life is designed to be continually guided by Jesus. He initiates and builds experiences for us to treasure and learn from.

    "King Solomon made himself a chariot of the wood of Lebanon. He made the pillars thereof of silver, the bottom thereof of gold, the covering of it of purple, the midst thereof being paved with love, for the daughters of Jerusalem." Song of Solomon 3:9-10

4. God is love and His desire is towards us. He delights in knowing us and He knows all that is in us. Jesus thinks you are special and beyond compare.

"Thou hast ravished my heart, my sister, my spouse; thou hast ravished my heart with one of thine eyes, with one chain of thy neck. How fair is thy love, my sister, my spouse! how much better is thy love than wine! and the smell of thine ointments than all spices! Thy lips, O my spouse, drop as the honeycomb: honey and milk are under thy tongue; and the smell of thy garments is like the smell of Lebanon. A garden inclosed is my sister, my spouse; a spring shut up, a fountain sealed. Thy plants are an orchard of pomegranates, with pleasant fruits; camphire, with spikenard, Spikenard and saffron; calamus and cinnamon, with all trees of frankincense; myrrh and aloes, with all the chief spices: A fountain of gardens, a well of living waters, and streams from Lebanon. Awake, O north wind; and come, thou south; blow upon my garden, that the spices thereof may flow out. Let my beloved come into his garden, and eat his pleasant fruits." Song of Solomon 4:9-16

5. Jesus wants you to spend your time with Him. He wants you to meditate on His goodness and look for Him in all you do. He is our first love.

"I am my beloved's, and his desire is toward me. Come, my beloved, let us go forth into the field; let us lodge in the villages. Let us get up early to the vineyards; let us see if the vine flourish, whether the tender grape appear, and the pomegranates bud forth: there will I give thee my loves. The mandrakes give a smell, and at our gates are all manner of pleasant fruits, new and old, which I have laid up for thee, O my beloved." Song of Solomon 7:10-13

Making Jesus the most important and cherished part of our life leads us into a fruitful relationship with Him. Building for the kingdom has a momentum to it, but if we are not careful, we can be consumed with the building and forget our relationship with the One who called us to begin with. The favor to do what we are called to do has more to do with building relationship than it does about opportunity. We must keep Jesus a priority. We must remain delighted in all He is and all He offers. If every assignment you were trying to accomplish vanished, you would still have Jesus and that would still be an amazing, wonderful, adventurous life full of the blessings of God.

Jesus, I thank You for the favor You have poured out on my life. You have surrounded me with Your goodness and I am grateful that Your heart is the One I am after. I am thankful that You see me when I feel invisible. I pray to have eyes to see others and for the anointing that breaks the yoke of bondage to set others free. I repent for wanting to hoard You up for myself. Teach me to share Your goodness to those who need You most. Lord, let Your people be like a spring of water whose waters fail not. Let us never grow weary of seeking Your face and holding Your hand. It is in Your name I pray. Amen

"For thou, Lord, wilt bless the righteous; with favour wilt thou compass him as with a shield." Psalm 5:12

"For his anger endureth but a moment; in his favour is life: weeping may endure for a night, but joy cometh in the morning." Psalm 30:5

"Thou shalt arise, and have mercy upon Zion: for the time to favour her, yea, the set time, is come." Psalm 102:13

"And the Lord shall guide thee continually, and satisfy thy soul in drought, and make fat thy bones: and thou shalt be like a watered garden, and like a spring of water, whose waters fail not." Isaiah 58:11

-Jesus is the true source of our favor. Worldly favor tries to tempt us into thinking how well we are perceived comes from material goods, but true Godly favor comes from an obedient lifestyle to the Word of God and the amount of grace given to us in order to achieve our destiny.

-Favor does not always feel like favor. In fact, it is often wrapped in rejection. There are many Biblical examples of people being guided into their calling through the process of rejection.

-The prophet Balaam learned that God would only allow His people to be blessed, that is until they decided to disobey the Lord's commandments and do things they were told not to do. The blessings of God are given to His submitted children, but the rebellious take on His wrath. Gratefully, we live under a covenant of grace bought by Jesus at the cross, but we are still responsible for repenting of the sins that separate us from Jesus.

-Our relationship with Jesus is the corner stone to any opportunity that may come our way. If we keep Him front and center we will be satisfied with every door He opens.

PREPARED: LITTLE BY LITTLE

If you decided to run a marathon tomorrow how well would you do? If you are like me, you would not feel ready to take on a run of that magnitude. A race down the driveway is more my speed at the moment. I am simply not prepared mentally or physically to push myself that many miles.

Our walk with Jesus takes some preparation. The situations we encounter require some training and gleaning in advance. The great part of walking with the Creator of the Universe is that He knows this about us. He knows the exact amount we are able to take on. He knows what will stretch us but not leave us broken. Romans 5:3-4 tells us, "And not only so, but we glory in tribulations also: knowing that tribulation worketh patience; And patience, experience; and experience, hope:"

A season of tribulation produces patience. A season of patience produces experience. A season of experience produces hope. One season always gives way to another season, preparing us for the days ahead. We may not be able to run a marathon tomorrow, but if we had a plan of attack, a way to build on each attempt, we could get there. We would run our marathon and then wonder what challenge to take on next.

Proverbs tells us:

-"Go to the ant, thou sluggard; consider her ways, and be wise: Which having no guide, overseer, or ruler, Provideth her meat in the summer, and gathereth her food in the harvest." Proverbs 6:6-8

-"Prepare thy work without, and make it fit for thyself in the field; and afterwards build thine house." Proverbs 24:7

The Message version puts it this way:
"First plant your fields; then build your barn."

-"The ants are a people not strong, yet they prepare their meat in the summer;" Proverbs 30:25

When we consider the ant we learn:
1. Nobody has to tell them what to do or when.
2. They prepare in advance for what is to come.
3. Diligence and faithfulness are their strengths.

The Lord never gives us the fulness of what we are working towards all at once. It is always little by little. When God was telling the Israelites about the opposition to the land they would inherit, He told them, "I will not drive them out from before thee in one year; lest the land become desolate, and the beast of the field multiply against thee. By little and little I will drive them out from before thee, until thou be increased, and inherit the land" (Exodus 23:29-30).

God cleared the land for His people one piece at a time, giving them space to grow and the opportunity for them to learn how to steward the increase. You may be thinking, "What does this have to do with being prepared?" Well…as we increase in the Lord our skillsets grow. Our patience grows. Our character grows. The little by little feels frustrating to our flesh, but it helps our spirit man thrive.

An architect can make a building look like anything it wants. Houses come in all shapes, sizes, and features. Your commitment with the Lord is to build according to His blueprints. He sets the pace for construction, but we can halt the progress.

Do you remember Solomon's part of the deal? He was to:

-Build God's House and Courts
-Be Constant
-Do God's Commandments and Judgments
-Keep and Seek God's Commandments
-Possess the Land
-Know God
-Serve God with a Perfect Heart and a Willing Mind
-Be Strong and Do It

If we are to do this too, we must be like that little ant who is driven by the knowledge that preparation now equals big gains later. Benjamin Franklin once said, "An ounce of prevention is worth a pound of cure." Look at your life, where are you building for the future? If you are just getting started in your big adventure with the Lord, now is the time to make some commitments knowing what you do now will serve you later. If you have been at it a while and feel like you are spinning your wheels, know that it is never too late to push forwards. Everything you have done up to this point has prepared you for what is ahead.

In all this "getting ready," however, what we really need to keep in front of us is the preparation for eternity. What we do here and now matters, but it matters only in the context of who it helps and what is to come. What God is most interested in is preparing your soul for Him:

> Let us be glad and rejoice, and give honour to him: for the marriage of the Lamb is come, and his wife hath made herself ready. And to her was granted that she should be arrayed in fine linen, clean and white: for the fine linen is the righteousness of saints. And he saith unto me, Write, Blessed are they which are called unto the marriage supper of the Lamb. And he saith unto me, These are the true sayings of God.
>
> -Revelation 19:7-9

Just Enough

When my husband and I go out of town, I always overpack. I like to make sure we are ready for any situation, plus I want to have options. Having no options is stressful, having just enough options is freeing, and having too many options is overwhelming.

Jesus tells a parable about ten women who had just enough. They prepared in advance and when the time came they had enough to make it count:

> Then shall the kingdom of heaven be likened unto ten virgins, which took their lamps, and went forth to meet the bridegroom. And five of them were wise, and five were foolish. They that were foolish took their lamps, and took no oil with them: But the wise took oil in their

vessels with their lamps. While the bridegroom tarried, they all slumbered and slept. And at midnight there was a cry made, Behold, the bridegroom cometh; go ye out to meet him. Then all those virgins arose, and trimmed their lamps. And the foolish said unto the wise, Give us of your oil; for our lamps are gone out. But the wise answered, saying, Not so; lest there be not enough for us and you: but go ye rather to them that sell, and buy for yourselves. And while they went to buy, the bridegroom came; and they that were ready went in with him to the marriage: and the door was shut. Afterward came also the other virgins, saying, Lord, Lord, open to us. But he answered and said, Verily I say unto you, I know you not. Watch therefore, for ye know neither the day nor the hour wherein the Son of man cometh.

-Matthew 25:1-13

Jesus is telling us here that we have a certain amount of personal responsibility in our walk with Him. We must be able to lead our own life into His will for us. When God gave Adam the garden of Eden, He told him to name the animals. God gives us responsibilities and opportunities to grow and be obedient. Our lamps need to be full. It is our job to prepare what we need for His return. Remember, it is the bride who makes herself ready. Think about how much effort goes into a wedding. Every part of a wedding is prepared.

Nobody is going to do the work for you. Nobody is going to hand you a completed book. Nobody is going to grow your ministry. Nobody is going to finish your next project. You may get some help, praise God, but the majority of the responsibility to DO the work lies on your shoulders. You are the one He has called. You are the one who carries your cross. Plan in advance what you need as much as you can, seek out the Lord for a strategy, and get to work. If an ant can do it, so can you!

That Same Hour

Okay…I am going to counter what I just said with the opposite advice. Sounds strange, but the kingdom works that way sometimes. Jesus calls us to be prepared, instant in season and out, but He also tells us to be completely dependent on Him. It is essential that we know the voice of the Lord. We want to hear His still, small voice, while also being able to recognize the times the Spirit grabs a hold of us and shakes us to our core. Hearing from God is a daily part of our relationship. Prayer is how you prepare in advance for something you could never do yourself. Staying in the Word keeps your lamp lit. Keeping yourself in the house of God gives you a tender heart to receive. The lifestyle of a believer is one way we prepare for the impossible that only God can do.

Receiving the gift of the Holy Ghost was the turning point in my relationship with Jesus. I went from someone who followed Jesus, to someone who fervently sought Him out- not because I am great, but because He is great. Romans 5:5 tells us, "And hope maketh not ashamed; because the love of God is shed abroad in our hearts by the Holy Ghost which is given unto us." Jesus, our bridegroom, wants us to be ready for Him. It is in Him, through Him, because of Him, and for Him that we walk this walk listening for the sound of His voice. It is His voice that we follow, not man's and not the world's, only the sweet sound of Jesus:

> My sheep hear my voice, and I know them, and they follow me: And I give unto them eternal life; and they shall never perish, neither shall any man pluck them out of my hand.
>
> -John 10:27-28

I cannot emphasize enough the importance of prayer in your building. Council is good, but people will unknowingly steer you wrong. You cannot depend on someone's opinion to guide you. The confirmation on what to do and say must come from the One who wrote the blueprint. If you are panicking a bit because this sounds hard, relax. If we keep our lamps lit, we will hear our Shephard's voice. Jesus warns of a time when hearing Him and speaking His words becomes very important:

> Behold, I send you forth as sheep in the midst of wolves: be ye therefore wise as serpents, and harmless as doves. But beware of men: for they will deliver you up to the councils, and they will scourge you in their synagogues; And ye shall be brought before governors and kings for my sake, for a testimony against them and the Gentiles. But when they deliver you up, take no thought how or what ye shall speak: for it shall be given you in that same hour what ye shall speak. For it is not ye that speak, but the Spirit of your Father which speaketh in you.
>
> -Matthew 10:16-20

What we are building and what we are being prepared for is a life of serving. Jesus came to serve. He bore our sins, carried our burdens, and took stripes for our healing. His heart is for others. Romans 12:3 tells us, "For I say, through the grace given unto me, to every man that is among you, not to think of himself more highly than he ought to think; but to think soberly, according as God hath dealt to every man the measure of faith." Sometimes it is hard to remember that the call on our lives is not about us. We can be so caught up in the work that it becomes self-centered and we forget the reason God called us to begin with. Even the disciples had this dilemma:

> And James and John, the sons of Zebedee, come unto him, saying, Master, we would that thou shouldest do for us whatsoever we shall desire. And he said unto them, What would ye that I should do for you? They said unto him, Grant unto us that we may sit, one on thy right hand, and the other on thy left hand, in thy glory. But Jesus said unto them, Ye know not what ye ask: can ye drink of the cup that I drink of? and be baptized with the baptism that I am baptized with? And they said unto him, We can. And Jesus said unto them, Ye shall indeed drink of the cup that I drink of; and with the baptism that I am baptized withal shall ye be baptized: But to sit on my right hand and on my left hand is not mine to give; but it shall be given to them for whom it is prepared.
>
> -Mark 10:35-40

Jesus told James and John that the positions they were after had been prepared for the one who was called to it. This is freedom for the builder. We don't have to wiggle our way into position. We don't have to strive or struggle. Our job is to walk with Jesus, go where He leads us, and serve. Serve the sick. Serve the hurting. Serve the lonely. Serve the hungry. When you look at your building, ask yourself "Who am I serving?"

James and John received this revelation the hard way. They had to walk through it and be the set-up for the example. This didn't make Jesus love them less. It was simply part of their role in the kingdom. We are all sometimes the non-example (the opposite example of what we are supposed to do), but through the grace of God we learn from it and continue down the path of righteousness. There is always grace for us in Christ Jesus. A little truth bomb here…there is not always grace in others. Friends, co-workers, family, church family, and others may not see you through eyes of grace, but Jesus will be there to help and give the lesson:

> And when the ten heard it, they began to be much displeased with James and John. But Jesus called them to him, and saith unto them, Ye know that they which are accounted to rule over the Gentiles exercise lordship over them; and their great ones exercise authority upon them. But so shall it not be among you: but whosoever will be great among you, shall be your minister: And whosoever of you will be the chiefest, shall be servant of all. For even the Son of man came not to be ministered unto, but to minister, and to give his life a ransom for many.
>
> -Mark 10:41-45

Advancing in the kingdom always comes from a heart that wants to serve. Ambition is a struggle (yes, I said struggle and if you are reading this book then you probably understand what I mean…ambition is a driving force all on its own that must be submitted to the Lord. Otherwise, ambition will lead you. Ambition will be your guide. Ambition will be the reason you get up in the morning. Ambition will be the idol you serve). Jesus cares about us enough to show us our true motivations and sometimes it isn't pretty. Sometimes what we want to achieve is rooted in self. It takes a work of the Spirit to break this deeply rooted need to be great. Have you examined yourself? Have you asked the Lord to search you? Do this now before you go any further.

In the book of Matthew, Jesus tells us the parable of the talents. He tells us no matter the number of talents we have been given, it is up to us to use them for His kingdom and draw interest by doing good works. Not coincidently He tells us that when we do good works for others it is as though we are doing them for Him too. This isn't a small lesson, it is perhaps one of the greatest lessons outside of salvation:

> And before him shall be gathered all nations: and he shall separate them one from another, as a shepherd divideth his sheep from the goats: And he shall set the sheep on his right hand, but the goats on the left. Then shall the King say unto them on his right hand, Come, ye blessed of my Father, inherit the kingdom prepared for you from the foundation of the world: For I was an hungred, and ye gave me meat: I was thirsty, and ye gave me drink: I was a stranger, and ye took me in: Naked, and ye clothed me: I was sick, and ye visited me: I was

in prison, and ye came unto me. Then shall the righteous answer him, saying, Lord, when saw we thee an hungred, and fed thee? or thirsty, and gave thee drink? When saw we thee a stranger, and took thee in? or naked, and clothed thee? Or when saw we thee sick, or in prison, and came unto thee? And the King shall answer and say unto them, Verily I say unto you, Inasmuch as ye have done it unto one of the least of these my brethren, ye have done it unto me. Then shall he say also unto them on the left hand, Depart from me, ye cursed, into everlasting fire, prepared for the devil and his angels: For I was an hungred, and ye gave me no meat: I was thirsty, and ye gave me no drink: I was a stranger, and ye took me not in: naked, and ye clothed me not: sick, and in prison, and ye visited me not. Then shall they also answer him, saying, Lord, when saw we thee an hungred, or athirst, or a stranger, or naked, or sick, or in prison, and did not minister unto thee? Then shall he answer them, saying, Verily I say unto you, Inasmuch as ye did it not to one of the least of these, ye did it not to me. And these shall go away into everlasting punishment: but the righteous into life eternal.
-Matthew 25:32-46

Jesus expects big things out of His followers. Big acts of maturity. Big acts of selflessness. Big lives laid down to serve.

Jesus, I thank You for the beauty of a submitted heart. Please take away anything that is not focused on the simple gospel of Jesus Christ. I repent for straying away. I repent for putting my eyes on the things of this world. Help me to look always for Your return. Help me to build in a way that tells the world they have a Savior who is returning. I believe You in this season. I believe You for Your promises on my life. I believe You for the abundance of riches that You carry- heavenly riches stored up for those You love. I will be confident in who You are and prepared to spend eternity worshipping at Your feet. It is in Your name I pray. Amen

"But sanctify the Lord God in your hearts: and be ready always to give an answer to every man that asketh you a reason of the hope that is in you with meekness and fear:" 1 Peter 3:15

"And now, little children, abide in him; that, when he shall appear, we may have confidence, and not be ashamed before him at his coming." 1 John 2:28

"Was not Abraham our father justified by works, when he had offered Isaac his son upon the altar? Seest thou how faith wrought with his works, and by works was faith made perfect? And the scripture was fulfilled which saith, Abraham believed God, and it was imputed unto him for righteousness: and he was called the Friend of God. Ye see then how that by works a man is justified, and not by faith only. Likewise also was not Rahab the harlot justified by works, when she had received the messengers, and had sent them out another way? For as the body without the spirit is dead, so faith without works is dead also." James 2:21-26

-Being prepared is a work that is done through the Spirit of God, but it is also something we choose to participate in. God calls us to take hold of the gospel and work for the kingdom.

-Our increase comes little by little. God drives out the habits and strongholds that keep us down a little at a time. He is preparing us for the positions we are destined to and making us more effective leaders and servants.

-Jesus expects His children to be mature and to get things done. Prayer and relationship are our path to understanding, "And that servant, which knew his lord's will, and prepared not himself, neither did according to his will, shall be beaten with many stripes. But he that knew not, and did commit things worthy of stripes, shall be beaten with few stripes. For unto whomsoever much is given, of him shall be much required: and to whom men have committed much, of him they will ask the more" (Luke 12:47-48).

-The reason we are building is to serve Jesus and others. Ambition isn't enough. Setting goals and hitting them isn't enough. Fame sure isn't enough. It must be about serving others. Loving others is the driving force behind what we do. When we serve others, we serve Jesus.

EXCELLENCE: ABOVE AND BEYOND

When the people saw Jesus heal the sick, make the deaf to hear and the blind to see they were astonished. Mark 7:37 tells us they said, "…he hath done all things well." Jesus operated in a spirit of excellence. His way was the best way. To be excellent means to go above and beyond what is standard. When we build, we should do so with the idea that what we are doing is for the kingdom of God and should be done with care and attention to detail.

We serve an above and beyond God:

-When Jesus turned water into wine, it was the best wine. The people marveled at how good it was. (John 2:10)

-When the leper came to thank Jesus for healing him, the Lord decided to go a step further and make him whole. (John 5:15)

-When Jesus told Peter to cast his net on the right side of the boat, the net became so full that they were not able to draw it in. (John 21:6)

-When Jesus fed the five thousand there were twelve baskets full left over. (Matthew 14:20).

Excellence is in the details and the big picture. When God gave instructions on how to build the temple He was very specific. He discussed His desires for the building as a whole and each part within the bigger picture.

Let's look at His instructions for the curtains. Notice how detailed they are. He even gives directions on the stitching…our God is in every detail:

> Moreover thou shalt make the tabernacle with ten curtains of fine twined linen, and blue, and purple, and scarlet: with cherubims of cunning work shalt thou make them. The length of one curtain shall be eight and twenty cubits, and the breadth of one curtain four cubits: and every one of the curtains shall have one measure. The five curtains shall be coupled together one to another; and other five curtains shall be coupled one to another. And thou shalt make loops of blue upon the edge of the one curtain from the selvedge in the coupling; and likewise shalt thou make in the uttermost edge of another curtain, in the coupling of the second. Fifty loops shalt thou make in the one curtain, and fifty loops shalt thou make in the edge of the curtain that is in the coupling of the second; that the loops may take hold one of another. And thou shalt make fifty taches of gold, and couple the curtains together with the taches: and it shall be one tabernacle. And thou shalt make curtains of goats' hair to be a covering upon the tabernacle: eleven curtains shalt thou make. The length of one curtain shall be thirty cubits, and the breadth of one curtain four cubits: and the eleven curtains shall be all of one measure. And thou shalt couple five

curtains by themselves, and six curtains by themselves, and shalt double the sixth curtain in the forefront of the tabernacle. And thou shalt make fifty loops on the edge of the one curtain that is outmost in the coupling, and fifty loops in the edge of the curtain which coupleth the second. And thou shalt make fifty taches of brass, and put the taches into the loops, and couple the tent together, that it may be one. And the remnant that remaineth of the curtains of the tent, the half curtain that remaineth, shall hang over the backside of the tabernacle. And a cubit on the one side, and a cubit on the other side of that which remaineth in the length of the curtains of the tent, it shall hang over the sides of the tabernacle on this side and on that side, to cover it.

-Exodus 26:1-13

Friends, this is what it means for God to be in the middle of a plan. If He cares this much about what the curtains look like, how much more does He care about the ins-and-outs of your life? If your building feels like heavy lifting, step back and think about the God who clothes the lilies in splendor. He knows when a sparrow hits the ground. He is a God who knows every part of His creation, why do you think you are going at this alone? Does His excellence not apply to you, too? You can trust Him to care, "How excellent is thy lovingkindness, O God! therefore the children of men put their trust under the shadow of thy wings" (Psalms 36:7).

The book of Proverbs tells us:

-"Give her of the fruit of her hands; and let her own works praise her in the gates." Proverbs 31:31

-"Excellent speech becometh not a fool: much less do lying lips a prince." Proverbs 17:7

The Lord promises to go above and beyond what is expected for His followers, "Now unto him that is able to do exceedingly abundantly above all that we ask or think, according to the power that worketh in us," (Ephesians 3:20). It is that Holy Ghost power working in us and through us that keeps our nets full to overflow. We can expect this Jesus who doesn't just scrape by to offer us life and life more abundantly (John 10:10). In fact, Jesus said we would do even greater things than He did because of that power (John 14:12). God is excellent to us and through us!

There are many examples of God using a spirit of excellence to guide people into His will for their life:

Daniel

> There is a man in thy kingdom, in whom is the spirit of the holy gods; and in the days of thy father light and understanding and wisdom, like the wisdom of the gods, was found in him; whom the king Nebuchadnezzar thy father, the king, I say, thy father, made master of the magicians, astrologers, Chaldeans, and soothsayers; Forasmuch as an excellent spirit,

and knowledge, and understanding, interpreting of dreams, and shewing of hard sentences, and dissolving of doubts, were found in the same Daniel...

-Daniel 5:11-12

Joseph

And Joseph was brought down to Egypt; and Potiphar, an officer of Pharaoh, captain of the guard, an Egyptian, bought him of the hands of the Ishmeelites, which had brought him down thither. And the Lord was with Joseph, and he was a prosperous man; and he was in the house of his master the Egyptian. And his master saw that the Lord was with him, and that the Lord made all that he did to prosper in his hand. And Joseph found grace in his sight, and he served him: and he made him overseer over his house, and all that he had he put into his hand. And it came to pass from the time that he had made him overseer in his house, and over all that he had, that the Lord blessed the Egyptian's house for Joseph's sake; and the blessing of the Lord was upon all that he had in the house, and in the field. And he left all that he had in Joseph's hand; and he knew not ought he had, save the bread which he did eat. And Joseph was a goodly person, and well favoured.

-Genesis 39:1-6

So it came to pass, when the king's commandment and his decree was heard, and when many maidens were gathered together unto Shushan the palace, to the custody of Hegai, that Esther was brought also unto the king's house, to the custody of Hegai, keeper of the women. And the maiden pleased him, and she obtained kindness of him; and he speedily gave her her things for purification, with such things as belonged to her, and seven maidens, which were meet to be given her, out of the king's house: and he preferred her and her maids unto the best place of the house of the women…And Esther obtained favour in the sight of all them that looked upon her. So Esther was taken unto king Ahasuerus into his house royal in the tenth month, which is the month Tebeth, in the seventh year of his reign. And the king loved Esther above all the women, and she obtained grace and favour in his sight more than all the virgins; so that he set the royal crown upon her head, and made her queen instead of Vashti.

-Esther 2:8-17

What we learn from the examples of above and beyond is that excellence shows itself through character, gifts, and the way one is received:

1. God can be seen in the work
2. Godly wisdom, knowledge, and interpretation
3. Dissolving of doubts (an encouraging spirit)
4. The works of your hands prosper
5. Grace and trust with leaders
6. Others will be blessed because of you
7. A good spirit
8. Resources will be given to you
9. Special relationships
10. Supernatural positioning

Jesus wants us to do all things well and He also wants us to do them unto the Lord, "And whatsoever ye do, do it heartily, as to the Lord, and not unto men; Knowing that of the Lord ye shall receive the reward of the inheritance: for ye serve the Lord Christ" (Colossians 3:23-24). It is very easy to get caught up in competition and where we are going next, but the Lord doesn't want us to have any other agenda than to love Him and love others, to serve Him and serve others, and to honor Him and honor others. Our primary place of position is at His feet.

When Mary sat at Jesus' feet, she poured out the best oil. She worshipped by going above and beyond. There were barriers in her way, things that would have stopped her had she let them, but a spirit of excellence drove her forward:

> Then Jesus six days before the passover came
> to Bethany, where Lazarus was which had been

dead, whom he raised from the dead. There they made him a supper; and Martha served: but Lazarus was one of them that sat at the table with him. Then took Mary a pound of ointment of spikenard, very costly, and anointed the feet of Jesus, and wiped his feet with her hair: and the house was filled with the odour of the ointment. Then saith one of his disciples, Judas Iscariot, Simon's son, which should betray him, Why was not this ointment sold for three hundred pence, and given to the poor? This he said, not that he cared for the poor; but because he was a thief, and had the bag, and bare what was put therein.

-John 12:1-6

There will be people around you that say you should put your efforts elsewhere. They will say what you are doing is foolish. They will think you are wasting your time and energy, but don't let the opinions of others stop your building. If Mary had looked to Judas instead of Jesus for approval, she would have never had her life-changing experience. It's easy to be excellent when everyone is for you. It is a different thing all together to go above and beyond when others are calling you to maintain normalcy. Don't be like the man at the pool of Bethesda who laid there year after year because he had no man to put him in (John 5:1-14). Lean on Jesus, He will get you where you are supposed to be. He can make you whole in an instant- you might not need the pool you think you need! In fact, your miracle might be in a completely different way than what you are chasing after. Lean on Jesus, He will do it. In Psalm 26,

David writes that he will "walk in his integrity" even though there are others who walk in mischief:

> Lord, I have loved the habitation of thy house, and the place where thine honour dwelleth. Gather not my soul with sinners, nor my life with bloody men: In whose hands is mischief, and their right hand is full of bribes. But as for me, I will walk in mine integrity: redeem me, and be merciful unto me. My foot standeth in an even place: in the congregations will I bless the Lord.
>
> -Psalm 26:8-12

Mary took her best and gave it to God. What she did wasn't normal it was supernatural. Your building is going to require giant acts of faith that will cost you something. It cost Mary her concern for her reputation, her finances, and her sense of what was acceptable. Don't let culture keep you from moving closer to Jesus. Don't let your reputation keep you from moving closer to Jesus. Don't let fear of man keep you from moving closer to Jesus. Daniel, Joseph, and Esther were called to the big leagues. They dealt with kings and held the future of others in their hands. The big calls of God are for those who are willing to give it all up to do what is right in the sight of the Lord. These pioneers are willing to go above and beyond their neighbors and friends. They have a desire to see God work in ways that can only be achieved by putting it all on the line. How much are you willing to risk to see Jesus pull through for you?

There was a young man in the book of Matthew who was practically perfect in every way. He had done everything the right way according to the law, but something still had hold of him. Jesus knew that if this man was to be free he had to make a big move. The catalyst to following Jesus would be a giant leap of faith, losing one thing to gain everything:

> Jesus said unto him, If thou wilt be perfect, go and sell that thou hast, and give to the poor, and thou shalt have treasure in heaven: and come and follow me. But when the young man heard that saying, he went away sorrowful: for he had great possessions.
>
> -Matthew 19:21-23

The Lord wants us to be blessed, but He also wants us to walk with our hands open. When faced with great loss Job said, "…Naked came I out of my mother's womb, and naked shall I return thither: the Lord gave, and the Lord hath taken away; blessed be the name of the Lord" (Job 1:21).

What are you holding onto that the Lord can't have?

My son works as a cashier in an auto shop. He came home one evening, pulled some change out of his pocket, and said, "Someone just gave me their change. There are so many people who don't want their change." He couldn't believe there were people in the world who didn't value the coins he so carefully stored in a huge glass jug in his room.

The next day I was checking out at the grocery store when a few pennies fell from my hand onto the floor. I bent over to pick them up and heard the Lord say, "Do you want your change?" It hit me like a ton of bricks. I had been praying for outcomes that would require major changes in my life and yet I was fearful of what that life would look like after they came. What would it mean to be a die-hard, all or nothing, above and beyond follower of Christ? I was upset because it seemed I had lost so much of my old self in the pursuit, yet that was exactly what I wanted- to be a new creation. I was acting as though I didn't want my change.

I don't know how much you repent, but I have to do it a lot. Repentance isn't a punishment for the wicked, it is a way of life for those who wish to be as close to God as possible. Sin separates us, but repentance cleanses us and draws us closer to holiness. I repented that moment for my attitude and my fear. I repented for not giving Jesus the benefit of the doubt and believing Him for every promise. I repented for my lack of joy. I wanted change, but I wasn't happy about the in-between. I wasn't happy about going through hard things. I wasn't happy that change required a process, that it wasn't simple, and it wasn't the way I would have done it. I was mourning the loss of dreams and the lifestyle I used to live. The refining fire had shown me a weakness that I was blaming God for. I thought He was slow to move for me, but it turned out I was slow to trust.

If the practically perfect young man in the book of Matthew would have trusted Jesus with everything, his life would have drastically changed. He could have experienced first-hand the wonder of God in flesh working miracles on behalf of man. He could have seen the sick healed, the deaf to hear, the blind to see, and the dead to live. He could have been a helper to God. His life would have been historic. And yet he settled for what he knew. He settled for his wealth, his reputation, and his comfort. He could have lost everything and gained it all, but instead, he lost his privilege to walk with Jesus and gained regret. I wonder how many times he looked back at that moment and thought about how his life could have been different if only he had wanted his change.

What are you holding onto that the Lord can't have and is it more valuable than what He has to offer?

- "…let us lay aside every weight, and the sin which doth so easily beset us, and let us run with patience the race that is set before us," Hebrews 12:1

- "But seek ye first the kingdom of God, and his righteousness; and all these things shall be added unto you." Matthew 6:33

-"Let love be without dissimulation. Abhor that which is evil; cleave to that which is good." Romans 12:9

-"Lay not up for yourselves treasures upon earth, where moth and rust doth corrupt, and where thieves break through and steal: But lay up for yourselves treasures in heaven, where neither moth nor rust doth corrupt, and where thieves do not break through nor steal: For where your treasure is, there will your heart be also." Matthew 6:19-21

-"The light of the body is the eye: if therefore thine eye be single, thy whole body shall be full of light." Matthew 6:22

Giving up what we think we want for a kingdom-minded mission stirs up the gift of excellence in our life. Keeping our eyes focused on Jesus causes us to want do things well. We take into account every piece of the puzzle and know every part of our mission matters. Every soul. Every prayer. Every nail in the building is important.

Jesus, I thank You for doing all things well. Everything You put Your hands to is wonderful. I trust You to take care of me. Help me to rest in the comfort of Your shadow. Let it be a place of safety from the cares of this world. I repent for thinking I was the one who made myself good. I realize now it is only by the grace of God I am able to move in excellence. All good gifts come from above and I am grateful for every last one of them. I pray for the best gifts to flow in the body of Christ. Please allow Your gifts to manifest so others may see them and be thankful that there is a God in heaven who gives such good gifts to His children. It is in Your name I pray. Amen

"Finally, brethren, whatsoever things are true, whatsoever things are honest, whatsoever things are just, whatsoever things are pure, whatsoever things are lovely, whatsoever things are of good report; if there be any virtue, and if there be any praise, think on these things." Philippians 4:8

"Forasmuch as an excellent spirit, and knowledge, and understanding, interpreting of dreams, and shewing of hard sentences, and dissolving of doubts, were found in the same Daniel, whom the king named Belteshazzar: now let Daniel be called, and he will shew the interpretation." Daniel 5:12

"How excellent is thy lovingkindness, O God! Therefore the children of men put their trust under the shadow of thy wings." Psalm 36:7

-To be excellent is to go above and beyond what is standard. Jesus did all things well. He is the God of more than and when He breathes on a situation it is an over the top, more than you could imagine, only God could do it solution.

-The spirit of excellence will guide us into God's will for our lives. Excellence opens doors. Daniel, Joseph, and Esther were positioned because of the excellence they demonstrated.

-Sometimes others will not understand what we pour out to the Lord. When Mary broke the box and anointed Jesus, there were those who thought she was foolish. Only you know what God has put in you to do. This is why the opinion of man is dangerous to our call. If we lean too heavily on someone else's opinion we will flow with what they think is right rather than what God wants us to do. God wants our best and sometimes the return the world would call successful would be the very thing that would stop us from serving Him.

-Serving God means being completely focused on the way is excellent will of God for our lives. We have to want the change He is offering us. When we start to build with the Lord we willingly give up everything that has a hold on us to do things His way.

HONOR: THE BUILDER'S HOUSE

If we revisit the beginning chapter of this book, we remember God has chosen us to build with Him. We are walking ministries, ready hands and feet longing to help others come closer to Jesus. What we do and say is a reflection of the relationship we have with our Lord. Our house matters because it reflects the One who built us. His name is on the line. It is the name of Jesus that covers us, therefore, we submit our will to His will and do things His way. Paul called our work in a profession. Professionals take what they do seriously. Professionals study to show themselves approved. Professionals are careful with their words. They want to honor their employer and do well. When we receive honor is it actually God who gets the glory for the life He has built:

> Wherefore, holy brethren, partakers of the heavenly calling, consider the Apostle and High Priest of our profession, Christ Jesus; Who was faithful to him that appointed him, as also Moses was faithful in all his house. For this man was counted worthy of more glory than Moses, inasmuch as he who hath builded the house hath more honour than the house. For every house is builded by some man; but he that built all things is God. And Moses verily was faithful in all his house, as a servant, for a testimony of those things which were to be spoken after; But Christ as a son over his own house; whose house are we, if we hold fast the confidence and the rejoicing of the hope firm unto the end.
>
> -Hebrews 3:1-6

Look at your life. What is God building? Where has He placed you? Who are your influences? There are people around you that are already walking in what you are also called to walk in. God wants you to see them and learn from them. He is honoring others by putting you in their lives. He is telling them "I trust you with this lamb. Your ways please me and I would like you to teach them what I have taught you." We are called to serve God by teaching and also being teachable.

This is what the book of Proverbs has to say about honor:

-"Honour the Lord with thy substance, and with the firstfruits of all thine increase." Proverbs 3:9

-"The fear of the Lord is the instruction of wisdom; and before honour is humility." Proverbs 15:33

-"Before destruction the heart of man is haughty, and before honour is humility." Proverbs 18:12

-"It is an honour for a man to cease from strife: but every fool will be meddling." Proverbs 20:3

-"He that followeth after righteousness and mercy findeth life, righteousness, and honour." Proverbs 21:21

-"By humility and the fear of the Lord are riches, and honour, and life." Proverbs 22:4

-"A man's pride shall bring him low: but honour shall uphold the humble in spirit." Proverbs 29:23

It is evident from the book of Proverbs that honor is something we strive for and something we find when we live a humble life seeking after the Lord. It is not something we should give ourselves, but something that is earned through relationship with Jesus and others.

Honor means to be held in high esteem. Jesus spoke to His disciples often about the last being first and we read that same line of thinking throughout the book of Proverbs. Humility and honor go together like a peanut butter and jelly sandwich. True honor is impossible without a humble spirit. Leaders are servants and put others above themselves.

The Lord will connect you with people to learn from. This may come through a book, social media, or some other outlet. There will be people in your church and work environment whose skills and characteristics you will have an opportunity to witness and take on. Your family is also a beautiful way to see the goodness of God and how He operates. I have a dad who works really hard, in fact he is the hardest worker I know. One day in prayer, the Lord told me "I work like your dad works, only more. I am always working for you." I understood that work equals love. Dads work to provide for their families and leave something behind when they are gone. Dads work because they are driven to give good gifts to their children. Our God works like that for us. The Lord gave me an example of how He is through my dad and said it is good. Perhaps you think your family isn't the best example to draw from, but I challenge you to pray and ask God to show you a window into His heart through the people around you. He may give you someone as an opposite example, but even that shows His love. The Word is always our reference point for finding out more about what we notice in others. Does it line up with the

Bible? If so, pray God blesses you with the same abilities. If not, pray for the person you saw it in and pray the opposite trait for yourself and them. God will show you what needs to be prayed for.

What we aren't supposed to do, however, is see something within a person that doesn't line up in the Word and judge ourselves as better. Jesus warns us in a parable about seeing ourselves higher than we ought to:

> And he spake this parable unto certain which trusted in themselves that they were righteous, and despised others: Two men went up into the temple to pray; the one a Pharisee, and the other a publican. The Pharisee stood and prayed thus with himself, God, I thank thee, that I am not as other men are, extortioners, unjust, adulterers, or even as this publican. I fast twice in the week, I give tithes of all that I possess. And the publican, standing afar off, would not lift up so much as his eyes unto heaven, but smote upon his breast, saying, God be merciful to me a sinner. I tell you, this man went down to his house justified rather than the other: for every one that exalteth himself shall be abased; and he that humbleth himself shall be exalted.
>
> -Luke 18:9-14

The message here is clear, the tolerance we have for pride within ourselves should be very low. We honor God by loving His children, the ones He died for on the cross- all of them, not just the ones we like. When we look at someone who drives us a bit crazy, it is good for us to remember Jesus died for them, too. There will be people in the process of our building that we want to get away from, I think that is human nature and part of life. I also believe God puts people like that in our life to sharpen our love for others. It is easy to like people we naturally like. It is much harder to humble ourselves into a position where we have a genuine love for those who mock us or reject us. Don't worry, God will provide the humbling situations, you just have to make sure you don't jump ship before the heart change happens. Hang on and pray. Ask others to pray for you both. Wait on the Lord and He will make all the pieces come together. Keep your integrity while you wait- watch your words and your attitude. I'm speaking out of experience here, knowing I've been the person on both sides of the fence and wishing I had handled it better. I have seen people trying their best to like me and I had no idea what I was doing that was so unlikeable. I have also had to try my best to like others and fallen short on giving them grace. It was the gradual and loving humbling from the Lord that helped my heart see that person as a treasure and not a torment. This is a tough path to walk down, but Jesus holds our hand the whole way and knows the outcome is good.

Matthew 10:25 tells us it is enough for a servant to be like his master, meaning we will not be Jesus, but we can be like Him. We will not be exactly like our influences, but we can be like them. Pull the best traits from those around you and pray God gives you a portion. If it is your family, pray for generational blessings and callings to be gifted your way.

Examples in the Word where God gifts someone as an influence to His people:

-The Israelite women following Miriam out of bondage. (Exodus 15:15)

-Samuel ministering to the Lord before Eli. (1 Samuel 3:1)

-Elisha wearing Elijah's mantle. (2 Kings 2:13)

-The disciples calling Jesus their teacher. (John 13:13)

Those around you are your biggest influences. This is why it matters how you spend your time. If you spend your time doing secular things, you will pick up secular ways of thinking. As we discussed, manmade strategies won't cut it when you are looking for the anointing of God. You need divine strategies that are found through a separated lifestyle. God gives honor to those who seek after Him in all they do. Part-time Christianity isn't enough. The Lord knows our motives, He knows the time we spend getting to know Him better, and He knows if we are serious about having a life in Christ. We need to offer Him a full-time commitment. What does it mean to be separate? It means to live in fellowship with the body of Christ, to be a witness to the lost, and to keep ourselves on the straight and narrow. The straight and narrow drives out distraction from the purpose we are walking in. The straight and narrow keeps us in the will of God. The straight and narrow brings clarity to our life and gives Jesus the time He wants to spend with us. We want to follow Jesus as He leads, but also lead ourselves so we can help lead others. Leadership starts with honoring God's way of doing things. Matthew 7:14 tells us, "Because strait is the gate, and narrow is the way, which leadeth unto life, and few there be that find it." The apostle Paul guides us into God's heart for honoring those who are hard to love:

-"For I say, through the grace given unto me, to every man that is among you, not to think of himself more highly than he ought to think; but to think soberly, according as God hath dealt to every man the measure of faith." Romans 12:3

-"Be kindly affectioned one to another with brotherly love; in honour preferring one another;" Romans 12:10

-"Bless them which persecute you: bless, and curse not." Romans 12:14

-"Dearly beloved, avenge not yourselves, but rather give place unto wrath: for it is written, Vengeance is mine; I will repay, saith the Lord. Therefore if thine enemy hunger, feed him; if he thirst, give him drink: for in so doing thou shalt heap coals of fire on his head. Be not overcome of evil, but overcome evil with good." Romans 12:19-21

-"Only let your conversation be as it becometh the gospel of Christ: that whether I come and see you, or else be absent, I may hear of your affairs, that ye stand fast in one spirit, with one mind striving together for the faith of the gospel;" Philippians 1:27

-"Let nothing be done through strife or vainglory; but in lowliness of mind let each esteem other better than themselves." Philippians 2:3

-"Do all things without murmurings and disputings: That ye may be blameless and harmless, the sons of God, without rebuke, in the midst of a crooked and perverse nation, among whom ye shine as lights in the world;" Philippians 2:14-15

-"Let your speech be always with grace, seasoned with salt, that ye may know how ye ought to answer every man." Colossians 4:6

We honor God best when we follow His commandments, showing His love to every soul whether we think they deserve it or not. After all, we are all just sinners covered in the blood of Christ. Who are we to say one person is worthy of honor and another isn't? In 1 Corinthians 12:23, Paul reminds us that the parts of the body we consider less honorable are the parts that receive the most honor. We must become less so Jesus can be more. Let's make our pride small. Our judgements small. Our offenses small. But our words rich and meaningful, focused on the grace of God and pouring ourselves out over all He has built.

Jesus, I thank you for Your mercy and Your lovingkindness. You are the eternal God who deserves all the honor and all the glory. There is no God other than you. Your name Jesus is higher than every name. It is Your name that brings life and healing. Help me to minister grace to others. Help me to speak words of encouragement and life over everyone I meet. Help me to deal with situations and people that eat at my flesh. Lord, I want to walk in the Spirit and not in my own flesh. I want to cleave to Your way of doing things and turn the other cheek. Build something beautiful out of my mistakes and hurts. Help me to be fervent and diligent. Bless those who persecute me. It is in Your name I pray. Amen

"Now unto the King eternal, immortal, invisible, the only wise God, be honour and glory for ever and ever. Amen." 1 Timothy 1:17

"Let love be without dissimulation. Abhor that which is evil; cleave to that which is good. Be kindly affectioned one to another with brotherly love; in honour preferring one another; Not slothful in business; fervent in spirit; serving the Lord; Rejoicing in hope; patient in tribulation; continuing instant in prayer; Distributing to the necessity of saints; given to hospitality." Romans 12:9-13

"Honour all men. Love the brotherhood. Fear God. Honour the king." 1 Peter 2:17

-How we treat others is a reflection of our relationship with Jesus. We honor God best by honoring His children.

-Become teachable. Those around you are the biggest influences in your life. Are they the influences God chose for you? Do they lead you into pleasant places? Think about who and what you are filling your life with. Do your choices honor God's desire for your life? Watch what those around you are doing and saying. Learn from them. Pray for the good to be increased and demonstrated in your life. For those whose actions do not line up with the Word- don't do what they do- learn from their mistakes and pray for them.

-Keep your eyes on the straight and narrow path. It may look enticing to visit the worldly side for a bit, but make sure you don't get sucked into what the world says will work. You need divine strategy that is found through relationship with Jesus. Prayer. The Word. Worship. Fellowship. This is how you are driven down the path of God's will. Honor the process with righteousness.

-Speak honorable words to everyone. Those you like and those you don't. Be even more gracious to the people who are causing you problems. Try doing things God's way. Don't gossip. Don't slander. Don't backbite. Walk in your integrity and let God fight for your reputation.

THE SWEET SOUND OF "WELL DONE"

I recently visited a church for the first time and was given a tour by the Pastor and his wife. As I was taken around the campus, I heard the stories that came along with the building. How the pews had come from up North and were driven back by a truck driver who just happened to have an empty trailer. How the carpet had been donated and the rock fountain was built by someone in the church. How they found a creek on the property they never knew existed until a church member started pulling away at overgrown vines. There were so many stories that accompanied the property, and each told with love for the building that was built one piece at a time by their own hands. I could hear the heart of the congregation through the very structure of the church.

I believe this is how it is with what Jesus is building in us and through us. We are, after all, His temple which was bought at a very high price. Surely our God wouldn't just haphazardly throw us together and hope we stick. Think about how much care an earthly parent goes to for their kids to be successful. We take them to school. Make sure they remember what they need. Buy them all their necessities. Try to help them with their problems. Rejoice with them in their success. Guide them on the straight and narrow (as much as possible). Pray for them without ceasing. There is so much that goes into being a parent, and yet our love for our children is nothing compared to the Lord's love for us. It is almost impossible to fathom. There is something in us that wants to worry if we are doing this all right. Are we making the right moves, aligning ourselves with the right people, saying the right thing, or doing enough work to get the job done? But what if the real measure of success has nothing to do with how many followers you have, how big your building is, or even how much money you have in your bank account? What if success is measured by a heavenly standard that makes no sense to us here on earth.

It isn't bad to have followers or money, but it is dangerous to make them indicators of whether or not you are pleasing the Lord. Solomon had status, wealth, wisdom, and everything good under the sun, yet he lost his relationship with the One who really mattered. He allowed it all to go to his head and ended up with empty earthly treasures that moths and rust could corrupt (Matthew 6:19-20).

Jesus chose to make Himself a servant with no reputation and it was because of this He was exalted (Philippians 2:7-10). One day we will all stand in front of Jesus, and I hope to hear the sweet sound of His voice as He joyfully throws open His arms and sings "Well done!" I believe it is up to us to get with the Lord and determine what success looks like in His eyes. What is the measure of well done for the One who does all things well?

It is such a challenge not to get caught up in what the world says successful people look like. Jesus warns us, however, that "It is easier for a camel to go through the eye of a needle, than for a rich man to enter into the kingdom of God" (Matthew 19:24). It seems the very thing we desire on this earth is the very thing that makes it hard to spend eternity with Jesus. God wants to bless us, but He would rather keep us. Keeping our hearts tender before Him, listening for His voice, repenting for our sins, and loving the lost seem to be a far better effort than accumulating wealth and status. Perhaps true success looks more like this:

Matthew 25:32-46	Feed the hungry
	Give drink to the thirsty
	Clothe the naked
	Visit the sick and imprisoned
Mark 16:15-16	Preach the gospel
James 1:27	Visit the fatherless and widows
	Keep yourself unspotted

You were chosen to build for the Kingdom of God. You were chosen to drive back the darkness. You were chosen to seek the Lord's face and listen for His voice. You were chosen to do something amazing that only you can do. Be encouraged that God is for you and not against you. He wants you to succeed. He wants you to thrive. He wants you to have joy and life more abundantly. Keep Him first in all you do and watch Him turn your life into a treasure.

Reflection Questions:

1. How will you measure success?

    ____

    ____

    ____

    ____

2. What is your plan going forward to maintain relationship with Jesus?

    ____

    ____

    ____

    ____

3. Is there anyone you should pray for who might be losing their relationship for the sake of something else?

    ____

    ____

    ____

    ____

4. Where can you add more ministry into your life?

    ____

    ____

    ____

    ____

5. How has your idea of what it is to build with God changed?

    ____

    ____

    ____

    ____

-Solomon was given every worldly thing he asked for, but eventually lost it all because he lost his desire to seek God in all he did.

-How the world measures success and how God measures success are two completely different ways of thinking.

-It is up to us to seek out God's will for our lives. Jesus is the One who will tell us "Well done." He is the only heart that matters. Followers don't matter unless they matter to Jesus. Money doesn't matter unless it matters to Jesus. Status doesn't matter unless it matters to Jesus. The only thing we want is what Jesus wants for our lives. He knows best. It is His will and His way.

-Helping others, especially those who are the least likely to receive help, blesses the Kingdom of God. This is what we were always meant to be- helpers in the kingdom.

Ye are the salt of the earth: but if the salt have lost his savour, wherewith shall it be salted? it is thenceforth good for nothing, but to be cast out, and to be trodden under foot of men. Ye are the light of the world. A city that is set on an hill cannot be hid. Neither do men light a candle, and put it under a bushel, but on a candlestick; and it giveth light unto all that are in the house. Let your light so shine before men, that they may see your good works, and glorify your Father which is in heaven.

-Matthew 5:13-16

ABOUT THE AUTHOR

Ashley Ennis is a licensed minister through the Associated Brotherhood of Christians and editor of their publication *Our Herald*. She preaches at Victory Mission Bible Training Center in Center Ridge, Arkansas, a residential program for those overcoming life-controlling habits through the Word of God. She is also the Women's Minister and Social Media Director at her church, Plainview Jesus Name Church.

Ashley is blessed to work with her family on their farm, Ralston Family Farms. One of her biggest joys is the opportunity to help in their "Family to Family" rice donation program.

Website: www.ashleyennis.com